Traeger Grill & Smoker Cookbook

The Complete Wood Pellet Smoker and Grill Cookbook

Jarden Blardn

Table of contents

Introduction 6

Chapter 1: Traeger Wood Pellet Grill 101 7

What is Traeger Wood Pellet Grill? 7

Components of Traeger Wood Pellet Grill 7

How Does Traeger Wood Pellet Grill Work? 8

Traeger Wood Pellet Grill Vs. Charcoal And Wood Grills 9

Chapter 2: Tips for Successful Traeger Wood Pellet Grilling 10

Chapter 3: Common FAQs for Traeger Wood Pellet Grill 11

Chapter 4: Beef Recipes 13

BBQ Sweet Pepper Meatloaf 13

Blackened Steak 15

BBQ Brisket 16

Prime Rib Roast 17

Thai Beef Skewers 18

Cowboy Cut Steak 20

Grilled Butter Basted Steak 22

Chili Rib Eye Steaks 23

BBQ Beef Short Ribs 25

Thai Beef Salad 26

Chapter 5: Pork Recipes 28

Bacon-Wrapped Sausages in Brown Sugar 28

Sweet and Hot BBQ Ribs 29

Lemon Pepper Pork Tenderloin 30

Chinese BBQ Pork 31

Smoked Sausages 33

BBQ Baby Back Ribs 34

Roasted Whole Ham in Apricot Sauce 36

Pork Belly 37

Pulled Pork 38

Pork Steak 39

Chapter 6: Lamb Recipes 41

Roasted Leg of Lamb 41

Greek-Style Roast Leg of Lamb 43

Lamb Chops 45

Smoked Rack of Lamb 47

Rosemary Lamb 49

Lamb Chops with Rosemary and Olive oil 50

Boneless Leg of Lamb 51

Smoked Lamb Shoulder 53

Herby Lamb Chops 55

Garlic Rack of Lamb 57

Chapter 7: Poultry Recipes 59

Herb Roasted Turkey 59

Turkey Legs 61

Turkey Breast 63

HellFire Chicken Wings 65

Spicy BBQ Chicken 67

BBQ Half Chickens 68

Teriyaki Wings 69

Korean Chicken Wings 71

Garlic Parmesan Chicken Wings 73

Rosemary Orange Chicken 74

Chapter 8: Fish and Seafood Recipes 75

Jerk Shrimp 75

Spicy Shrimps Skewers 77

Lobster Tails 78

Lemon Garlic Scallops 80

Halibut in Parchment 82

Chilean Sea Bass 83

Sriracha Salmon 85

Grilled Rainbow Trout 87

Cider Salmon 88

Cajun Shrimp 90

Chapter 9: Game Recipes 91

Cornish Game Hens 91

BBQ Elk Short Ribs 92

Grilled Duck Breast 93

Bison Slider 94

Venison Rib Roast 95

Venison Meatloaf 96

Chapter 10: Vegetable Recipes **98**

Green Beans with Bacon 98

Grilled Potato Salad 99

Vegetable Sandwich.. 100

Grilled Zucchini.. 102

Grilled Sugar Snap Peas 103

Cauliflower with Parmesan and Butter.................................. 104

Grilled Carrots and Asparagus.. 105

Kale Chips 106

Roasted Root Vegetables 107

Vegetable Skewers 109

Conclusion 111

Introduction

A good barbecue consists of smoke, sizzles, and a great smell, all provided by effective use of the grill that someone has. The quality of the steaks and burger patties depends not only on the skills of the person making them but also is equally dependent on the equipment in use. Not many of us are barbecue experts who would know about what makes a grill better than others, but it can be a safe bet that if it minimizes the char and increases the overall flavor, it is something to look at.

Read on to know how to get started with scrumptious and fuss-free grilling journey.

Chapter 1: Traeger Wood Pellet Grill 101

What is Traeger Wood Pellet Grill?

Wood pellet grills are all the rage nowadays, and one of the best brands on the market is Traeger. Traeger Grills is a company in Oregon. It started when a person named Traeger choose to make a grill that would not fire up uncontrollably after one of his gas grills burnt. Now it has more than 6 models to its name with its sides of rubs and sauces. Their grill uses all-natural flavor woods or pellets as fuel.

Traeger wood pellet grills work with a motor moving a screw, which causes flames to increase or decrease by controlling the pellets' fire. The smoke and flames than go into a chimney, which reduces fire hazards and burning of the meat. The wood provides an extra level of taste, which makes a more sophisticated flavor profile making every dish more delicious. There are many flavors that woods can provide like cherry, apple, or pecan.

Components of Traeger Wood Pellet Grill

The grill comes in a compact and elegant design with each of its parts, having some function that ultimately makes your barbecuing experience more fun. There are eight main components of the machine which work together to provide you with results previously not in any other grilling device. The overall result of using Traeger wood pellet grills is better cooking of food, with more flavor and fewer mistakes.

The components are listed below:

- **Hardwood pallets**

These are the most important part of the grill. They function as the main fuel for the grill to work. All-natural hardwood flavorings can seep into your food while cooking through them. You can put any type of wood you want to bring a distinct taste to your dish.

- **Hopper**

This is where you will put your wood pellets in. The flavoring happens here as the wood ignites and cooks the food. 100% wood with no charcoal or gas connection required.

- **Controller**

The knob enables you to set the temperature of your choice and regulate it during the cooking process.

- **Induction Fan**

The fan turns on as you turn on the grill and heat up the food evenly by using the convection process for cooking. The Fan transfers hot air to the entirety of the grill, making it evenly distributed.

- **Auger**

It is a screw-like device that picks and places the wood pellets into the firepot to start the ignition process.

- **Hot rod**

This is where the pellets meet the fire and fire catches on. It is at the end of the auger.

- **Firepot**

Automatically fire is turned on, which ignites the hotrod and causes pellets to catch fire.

- **Drip Tray**

This piece of metal just above the fire prevents it from directly reaching the grill and reduces charring on food. It allows heat and smoke to pass through.

How Does Traeger Wood Pellet Grill Work?

The wood pellets are placed in the auger from the hopper. For higher temperatures, more wood pellets are added to the auger. The auger then transfers the wood pallets to the firepot where a fire is burning. The firepot makes the hotrod ignite the piece of wood, and smoke and fire from the wood are released. A drip tray stands just right on top of the hotrod and the burning wood to stops the naked flame. A fan inside the device is turned on, and it evenly distributes the smoke and heat to the food on top of the grill. For precise temperature controls, some grills are now equipped with an app that helps the cook control the temperature per his or her needs.

The Traeger wood pallets grill not only grills but also can be used for baking, smoking, roasting, and braising.

Traeger Wood Pellet Grill Vs. Charcoal and Wood Grills

Traeger wood pallets have numerous benefits that other charcoal and gas grill cannot provide. Barbecuing is a great gathering excuse and outdoor activity, but it is a hassle to set. In this day and age where everything is becoming more convenient, this activity should also become easier to deal with as well.

It is easy to start:

To get a charcoal or gas grill to ignite is a hassle, but the fire inside firepot is easy to turn on. It also is much safer as you don't have to stick your hands inside the grill to start the fire.

It's versatile

This grill is not only used for grilling but can be used for different processes of cooking as well. You can bake, roast, smoke, and braise using this device. This also increases the menu at your barbecue gathering.

No burnt areas

Because the cooking process happens by convection mechanism, the entire piece of meat, or whatever your cooking gets cooked evenly. There is also no need to flip around the meat constantly. Also, the drip tray prevents direct fire from hitting your food, so no charring occurs.

More flavor in your dishes

In grilling, nothing beats all-natural hardwood flavor. Professional chefs use them, and now, with ease, so could you. It is not hard to produce a much more delicious juicy meat steak at your home anymore.

Chapter 2: Tips for Successful Traeger Wood Pellet Grilling

The Traeger pellet grill is a great and somewhat expensive purchase. To make full use of it is your responsibility. Here are some tips for you to use your grill more effectively.

Use it as an oven

With the convection mechanism, the entirety of the grill gets an even distribution of heat and smoke. This makes it possible to be used as an oven. Let your imagination run wild with creative recipes you want to make or impress your friends with your unique culinary skills.

Use the pizza accessory

The pizza accessory is a must-have for those who love their grilling as much as their pizza. The three available types of heat settings for pizza are perfect. If you set the temperature, for example, 275° by the controller, then inside of the pizza stone can reach up to temperatures double that amount. Again, because of convection mechanism, even cooking of the pizza is ensured, and there is no charring at the bottom of the dough.

Put cold meat directly on low flames

Putting the smoking flavor in something thick as a brisket is very difficult. To achieve this, first, put your marinated pieces of meat on the heat directly from the fridge. Then set the temperature on low and wait for a while for them to be cooked. Increasing the time allows the smoke to transfer fully inside the meat, spreading it's a smoky flavor all over.

Use the upper racks

One of the great things in this grill is this upper rack to put food on top. It increases the amount of meat it can cook at one time and also increases storage. Most importantly, at the upper rack, temperatures are more controlled. Because the food is not directly on top of the hot slate, it ensures a more even cook.

Do reverse searing

It is a great way to cook pieces of meat, like steak. Put the meat on for a low flame to get a smoky flavor and then quickly change the settings to a higher amount. This method gives nice even medium-rare consistency in the meat.

Chapter 3: Common FAQs for Traeger Wood Pellet Grill

Question: What kind of pellets to use in the Traeger wood pellet grill?

Answer: Traeger wood pellet grill comes with its own brand of Traeger wood pallets to use along with it. You can use other wood pallets such as Q pallets to add your own flavoring to it, but it comes with a catch. The Traeger brand has said that if anyone uses other types and brands of wood apart of the Traeger, branded ones, then the warranty on the grill can be revoked. This may cause a lot of you to get anxious, but it is ok to use other types of pallets. There is a risk, but using other pallets such as Q pallets and cooking pallets are fine and enable you to stock up on them as well.

Question: How to start Traeger pellets smoker

Answer: Here is a step by step guide

- First, plug in your grill. The Traeger pellet grill is an electronic machine that needs a power outlet to work. Also, remove the grill trays, drip tray, and baffle.

- Then set the smoking temperature to your liking. It goes up to 180-200°F. You can adjust it by turning the dial.

- See that the auger is now moving. The wood is placed in the burner by the auger, so don't put the wood directly into the flames by hand.

- Check if it is burning up. DO NOT place your hand directly on the firepot because you will get burnt. As the flames turn on, a little smoke will start to generate in about 15 minutes, and also it will glow red, showing that the device is working.

- Put all the components of the grill back. Put the drip tray, grill trays, and baffle in their respective places.

- Put the pallets inside the hopper; the more you can fill the hopper, the better.

- Let it smoke for 1 minute on a high setting so that the entire grill gets seasoned.

Question: How to maintain your Traeger wood pellet grill?

Answer: Here are some ways to maintain and clean your Traeger grill

- It is important when using a wood pellet grill, you store your wood in a proper dry place. If moisture is accumulated than you left with nothing more than swelled up sawdust. Don't store the wood pallets in their box for too long, either. The entire should be used up with every barbecue session.

- You should cover your drip tray with a layer of aluminum foil so that cleaning is easier. If the drip tray ends up dirty anyway, then soak it in soapy water for about 15 minutes and then use a sponge to clean the food particles.
- You should clean your trays after every grilling session. When done, unplug the grill and wait till it cools down. After it has cooled, start to remove the grease.

Question: What to do if the temperature starts fluctuating?

Answer: First of all, don't panic as this can be normal. There are many reasons why this happens. The quality of the pallets may be poor, or the wind is blowing on the flames. The temperature is kept at an average by increasing and decreasing the flames, so fluctuations are normal.

Most of the time, if the temperature is seen to drop, it is because the auger stops delivering wood to the firepot.

It also can occur if the trays have become corroded over time.

Find the cause and try to fix it, or find answers through online support.

Chapter 4: Beef Recipes

BBQ Sweet Pepper Meatloaf

Preparation time: 20 minutes
Cooking time: 3 hours and 15 minutes
Servings: 8

Ingredients:

- 1 cup chopped red sweet peppers
- 5 pounds ground beef
- 1 cup chopped green onion
- 1 tablespoon salt
- 1 tablespoon ground black pepper
- 1 cup panko bread crumbs
- 2 tablespoon BBQ rub and more as needed
- 1 cup ketchup
- 2 eggs

Method:

1. Switch on the Traeger grill, fill the grill hopper with Texas beef blend flavored wood pellets, power the grill on by using the control panel, select 'smoke' on the temperature dial, or set the temperature to 225 degrees F and let it preheat for a minimum of 5 minutes.
2. Meanwhile, take a large bowl, place all the ingredients in it except for ketchup and then stir until well combined.
3. Shape the mixture into meatloaf and then sprinkle with some BBQ rub.
4. When the grill has preheated, open the lid, place meatloaf on the grill grate, shut the grill, and smoke for 2 hours and 15 minutes.
5. Then change the smoking temperature to 375 degrees F, insert a food thermometer into the meatloaf and cook for 45 minutes or more until the internal temperature of meatloaf reaches 155 degrees F.
6. Brush the top of meatloaf with ketchup and then continue cooking for 15 minutes until glazed.

7. When done, transfer food to a dish, let it rest for 10 minutes, then cut it into slices and serve.

Nutrition Value:

- Calories: 160.5 Cal
- Fat: 2.8 g
- Carbs: 13.2 g

- Protein: 17.2 g
- Fiber: 1 g

Blackened Steak

Preparation time: 10 minutes
Cooking time: 60 minutes
Servings: 4

Ingredients:

- 2 steaks, each about 40 ounces
- 4 tablespoons blackened rub
- 4 tablespoons butter, unsalted

Method:

1. Switch on the Traeger grill, fill the grill hopper with hickory flavored wood pellets, power the grill on by using the control panel, select 'smoke' on the temperature dial, or set the temperature to 225 degrees F and let it preheat for a minimum of 15 minutes.
2. Meanwhile, prepare the steaks and for this, sprinkle rub on all sides of each steak and let marinate for 10 minutes.
3. When the grill has preheated, open the lid, place steaks on the grill grate, shut the grill and smoke for 40 minutes until internal temperature reaches 119 degrees F.
4. When done, remove steaks from the grill and wrap each in a piece of foil.
5. Change the smoking temperature to 400 degrees F, place a griddle pan on the grill grate, and when hot, add 2 tablespoons butter and when it begins to melts, add steak and sear it for 4 minutes per side until internal temperature reaches 125 degrees F.
6. Transfer steaks to a dish and then repeat with the remaining steak.
7. Let seared steaks rest for 10 minutes, then slice each steak across the grain and serve.

Nutrition Value:

- Calories: 184.4 Cal
- Fat: 8.8 g
- Carbs: 0 g
- Protein: 23.5 g
- Fiber: 0 g

BBQ Brisket

Preparation time: 12 hours
Cooking time: 10 hours
Servings: 8

Ingredients:

- 1 beef brisket, about 12 pounds
- Beef rub as needed

Method:

1. Season beef brisket with beef rub until well coated, place it in a large plastic bag, seal it and let it marinate for a minimum of 12 hours in the refrigerator.
2. When ready to cook, switch on the Traeger grill, fill the grill hopper with hickory flavored wood pellets, power the grill on by using the control panel, select 'smoke' on the temperature dial, or set the temperature to 225 degrees F and let it preheat for a minimum of 15 minutes.
3. When the grill has preheated, open the lid, place marinated brisket on the grill grate fat-side down, shut the grill, and smoke for 6 hours until the internal temperature reaches 160 degrees F.
4. Then wrap the brisket in foil, return it back to the grill grate and cook for 4 hours until the internal temperature reaches 204 degrees F.
5. When done, transfer brisket to a cutting board, let it rest for 30 minutes, then cut it into slices and serve.

Nutrition Value:

- Calories: 328 Cal
- Fat: 21 g
- Carbs: 0 g
- Protein: 32 g
- Fiber: - g

Prime Rib Roast

Preparation time: 24 hours
Cooking time: 4 hours and 30 minutes
Servings: 8

Ingredients:

- 1 prime rib roast, containing 5 to 7 bones
- Rib rub as needed

Method:

1. Season rib roast with rib rub until well coated, place it in a large plastic bag, seal it and let it marinate for a minimum of 24 hours in the refrigerator.
2. When ready to cook, switch on the Traeger grill, fill the grill hopper with cherry flavored wood pellets, power the grill on by using the control panel, select 'smoke' on the temperature dial, or set the temperature to 225 degrees F and let it preheat for a minimum of 15 minutes.
3. When the grill has preheated, open the lid, place rib roast on the grill grate fat-side up, change the smoking temperature to 425 degrees F, shut the grill, and smoke for 30 minutes.
4. Then change the smoking temperature to 325 degrees F and continue cooking for 3 to 4 hours until roast has cooked to the desired level, rare at 120 degrees F, medium rare at 130 degrees F, medium at 140 degrees F, and well done at 150 degrees F.
5. When done, transfer roast rib to a cutting board, let it rest for 15 minutes, then cut it into slices and serve.

Nutrition Value:

- Calories: 248 Cal
- Fat: 21.2 g
- Carbs: 0 g
- Protein: 28 g
- Fiber: 0 g

Thai Beef Skewers

Preparation time: 15 minutes
Cooking time: 8 minutes
Servings: 6

Ingredients:

- ½ of medium red bell pepper, destemmed, cored, cut into a ¼-inch piece
- ½ of beef sirloin, fat trimmed
- ½ cup salted peanuts, roasted, chopped

For the Marinade:

- 1 teaspoon minced garlic
- 1 tablespoon grated ginger
- 1 lime, juiced
- 1 teaspoon ground black pepper
- 1 tablespoon sugar
- 1/4 cup soy sauce
- 1/4 cup olive oil

Method:

1. Prepare the marinade and for this, take a small bowl, place all of its ingredients in it, whisk until combined, and then pour it into a large plastic bag.
2. Cut into beef sirloin 1-1/4-inch dice, add to the plastic bag containing marinade, seal the bag, turn it upside down to coat beef pieces with the marinade and let it marinate for a minimum of 2 hours in the refrigerator.
3. When ready to cook, switch on the Traeger grill, fill the grill hopper with cherry flavored wood pellets, power the grill on by using the control panel, select 'smoke' on the temperature dial, or set the temperature to 425 degrees F and let it preheat for a minimum of 5 minutes.
4. Meanwhile, remove beef pieces from the marinade and then thread onto skewers.
5. When the grill has preheated, open the lid, place prepared skewers on the grill grate, shut the grill, and smoke for 4 minutes per side until done.
6. When done, transfer skewers to a dish, sprinkle with peanuts and red pepper, and then serve.

Nutrition Value:

- Calories: 124 Cal
- Fat: 5.5 g
- Carbs: 1.7 g

- Protein: 15.6 g
- Fiber: 0 g

Cowboy Cut Steak

Preparation time: 10 minutes
Cooking time: 1 hour and 15 minutes
Servings: 4

Ingredients:

- 2 cowboy cut steak, each about 2 ½ pounds
- Salt as needed
- Beef rub as needed

For the Gremolata:

- 2 tablespoons chopped mint
- 1 bunch of parsley, leaves separated
- 1 lemon, juiced
- 1 tablespoon lemon zest
- ½ teaspoon minced garlic
- ¼ teaspoon salt
- 1/8 teaspoon ground black pepper
- 1/4 cup olive oil

Method:

1. Switch on the Traeger grill, fill the grill hopper with mesquite flavored wood pellets, power the grill on by using the control panel, select 'smoke' on the temperature dial, or set the temperature to 225 degrees F and let it preheat for a minimum of 5 minutes.
2. Meanwhile, prepare the steaks, and for this, season them with salt and BBQ rub until well coated.
3. When the grill has preheated, open the lid, place steaks on the grill grate, shut the grill and smoke for 45 minutes to 1 hour until thoroughly cooked, and internal temperature reaches 115 degrees F.
4. Meanwhile, prepare gremolata and for this, take a medium bowl, place all of its ingredients in it and then stir well until combined, set aside until combined.

5. When done, transfer steaks to a dish, let rest for 15 minutes, and meanwhile, change the smoking temperature of the grill to 450 degrees F and let it preheat for a minimum of 10 minutes.
6. Then return steaks to the grill grate and cook for 7 minutes per side until the internal temperature reaches 130 degrees F.

Nutrition Value:

- Calories: 361 Cal
- Fat: 31 g
- Carbs: 1 g
- Protein: 19 g
- Fiber: 0.2 g

Grilled Butter Basted Steak

Preparation time: 10 minutes
Cooking time: 40 minutes
Servings: 2

Ingredients:

- 2 steaks, each about 16 ounces, 1 ½-inch thick
- Rib rub as needed
- 2 teaspoon Dijon mustard
- 2 tablespoons Worcestershire sauce
- 4 tablespoons butter, unsalted, melted

Method:

1. Switch on the Traeger grill, fill the grill hopper with hickory wood pellets, power the grill on by using the control panel, select 'smoke' on the temperature dial, or set the temperature to 225 degrees F and let it preheat for a minimum of 15 minutes.
2. Meanwhile, take a small bowl, place mustard, Worcestershire sauce, and butter in it and stir until well combined.
3. Brush the mixture on both sides of steaks and then season with rib rub.
4. When the grill has preheated, open the lid, place food on the grill grate, shut the grill, and smoke for 30 minutes.
5. When done, transfer steaks to a dish, let rest for 15 minutes, and meanwhile, change the smoking temperature of the grill to 450 degrees F and let it preheat for a minimum of 10 minutes.
6. Then return steaks to the grill grate and cook for 3 minutes per side until the internal temperature reaches 140 degrees F.
7. Transfer steaks to a dish, let rest for 5 minutes and then serve.

Nutrition Value:

- Calories: 409.8 Cal
- Fat: 30.8 g
- Carbs: 3.1 g
- Protein: 29.7 g
- Fiber: 0.4 g

Chili Rib Eye Steaks

Preparation time: 10 minutes
Cooking time: 1 hour
Servings: 4

Ingredients:

- 4 rib-eye steaks, each about 12 ounces

For the Rub:

- 1 tablespoon minced garlic
- 1 teaspoon salt
- 1 teaspoon brown sugar
- 2 tablespoons red chili powder
- 1 teaspoon ground cumin
- 2 tablespoons Worcestershire sauce
- 2 tablespoons olive oil

Method:

1. Prepare the rub and for this, take a small bowl, place all of its ingredients in it and then stir until mixed.
2. Brush the paste on all sides of the steak, rub well, then place steaks into a plastic bag and let it marinate for a minimum of 4 hours.
3. When ready to cook, switch on the Traeger grill, fill the grill hopper with mesquite flavored wood pellets, power the grill on by using the control panel, select 'smoke' on the temperature dial, or set the temperature to 225 degrees F and let it preheat for a minimum of 15 minutes.
4. When the grill has preheated, open the lid, place steaks on the grill grate, shut the grill, and smoke for 45 minutes until internal temperature reaches 120 degrees F.
5. When done, transfer steaks to a dish, let rest for 15 minutes, and meanwhile, change the smoking temperature of the grill to 450 degrees F and let it preheat for a minimum of 10 minutes.
6. Then return steaks to the grill grate and cook for 3 minutes per side until the internal temperature reaches 140 degrees F.
7. Transfer steaks to a dish, let rest for 5 minutes and then serve.

Nutrition Value:

- Calories: 293 Cal
- Fat: 0 g
- Carbs: 0 g
- Protein: 32 g
- Fiber: 0 g

BBQ Beef Short Ribs

Preparation time: 15 minutes
Cooking time: 10 hours
Servings: 8

Ingredients:

- 4 beef short rib racks, membrane removed, containing 4 bones
- 1/2 cup beef rub
- 1 cup apple juice

Method:

1. Switch on the Traeger grill, fill the grill hopper with apple-flavored wood pellets, power the grill on by using the control panel, select 'smoke' on the temperature dial, or set the temperature to 225 degrees F and let it preheat for a minimum of 15 minutes.
2. Meanwhile, prepare the ribs, and for this, sprinkle beef rub on both sides until well coated.
3. When the grill has preheated, open the lid, place ribs on the grill grate bone-side down, shut the grill, and smoke for 10 hours until internal temperature reaches 205 degrees F, spritzing with apple juice every hour.
4. When done, transfer ribs to a cutting board, let rest for 10 minutes, then cut into slices and serve.

Nutrition Value:

- Calories: 280 Cal
- Fat: 15 g
- Carbs: 17 g
- Protein: 20 g
- Fiber: 1 g

Thai Beef Salad

Preparation time: 10 minutes
Cooking time: 10 minutes
Servings: 4

Ingredients:

- 1 ½ pound skirt steak
- 1 ½ teaspoon salt
- 1 teaspoon ground white pepper

For the Dressing:

- 4 jalapeño peppers, minced
- ½ teaspoon minced garlic
- 4 tablespoons Thai fish sauce
- 4 tablespoons lime juice
- 1 tablespoon brown sugar

For the Salad:

- 1 small red onion, peeled, thinly sliced
- 6 cherry tomatoes, halved
- 2 green onions, ¼-inch diced
- 1 cucumber, deseeded, thinly sliced
- 1 heart of romaine lettuce, chopped
- ½ cup chopped mint
- 2 tablespoons cilantro
- ½ teaspoon red pepper flakes
- 1 tablespoon lime juice
- 2 tablespoons fish sauce

Method:

1. Switch on the Traeger grill, fill the grill hopper with cherry flavored wood pellets, power the grill on by using the control panel, select 'smoke' on the temperature

dial, or set the temperature to 450 degrees F and let it preheat for a minimum of 15 minutes.

2. Meanwhile, prepare the steak, and for this, season it with salt and black pepper until well coated.

3. When the grill has preheated, open the lid, place steak on the grill grate, shut the grill and smoke for 10 minutes until internal temperature reaches 130 degrees F.

4. Meanwhile, prepare the dressing and for this, take a medium bowl, place all of its ingredients in it and then stir until combined.

5. Take a large salad, place all the ingredients for the salad in it, drizzle with dressing and toss until well coated and mixed.

6. When done, transfer steak to a cutting board, let it rest for 10 minutes and then cut it into slices.

7. Add steak slices into the salad, toss until mixed, and then serve.

Nutrition Value:

- Calories: 128 Cal
- Fat: 6 g
- Carbs: 6 g
- Protein: 12 g
- Fiber: 1 g

Chapter 5: Pork Recipes

Bacon-Wrapped Sausages in Brown Sugar

Preparation time: 20 minutes
Cooking time: 30 minutes
Servings: 8

Ingredients:

- 1-pound bacon strips, halved
- 14 ounces cocktail sausages
- ½ cup brown sugar

Method:

1. Place bacon strips on clean working space, roll them by using a rolling pin, and then wrap a sausage with a bacon strip, securing with a toothpick.
2. Place wrapped sausage in a casserole dish, repeat with the other sausages, place them into the casserole dish in a single layer, cover with sugar and then let them sit for 30 minutes in the refrigerator.
3. When ready to cook, switch on the Traeger grill, fill the grill hopper with apple-flavored wood pellets, power the grill on by using the control panel, select 'smoke' on the temperature dial, or set the temperature to 350 degrees F and let it preheat for a minimum of 15 minutes.
4. Meanwhile, remove the casserole dish from the refrigerator and then arrange sausage on a cookie sheet lined with parchment paper.
5. When the grill has preheated, open the lid, place cookie sheet on the grill grate, shut the grill and smoke for 30 minutes.
6. When done, transfer sausages to a dish and then serve.

Nutrition Value:

- Calories: 270 Cal
- Fat: 27 g
- Carbs: 18 g
- Protein: 9 g
- Fiber: 2 g

Sweet and Hot BBQ Ribs

Preparation time: 10 minutes
Cooking time: 5 hours and 10 minutes
Servings: 4

Ingredients:

- 2 racks of pork ribs, bone-in, membrane removed
- 6 ounces pork and poultry rub
- 8 ounces apple juice
- 16 ounces sweet and heat BBQ sauce

Method:

1. Sprinkle pork and poultry rub on all sides of pork ribs until evenly coated, rub well and marinate for a minimum of 30 minutes.
2. When ready to cook, switch on the Traeger grill, fill the grill hopper with pecan flavored wood pellets, power the grill on by using the control panel, select 'smoke' on the temperature dial, or set the temperature to 225 degrees F and let it preheat for a minimum of 15 minutes.
3. When the grill has preheated, open the lid, place pork ribs on the grill grate bone-side down, shut the grill and smoke for 1 hour, spraying with 10 ounces of apple juice frequently.
4. Then wrap ribs in aluminum foil, pour in remaining 6 ounces of apple juice, and wrap tightly.
5. Return wrapped ribs onto the grill grate meat-side down, shut the grill and smoke for 3 to 4 hours until internal temperature reaches 203 degrees F.
6. Remove wrapped ribs from the grill, uncover it and then brush well with the sauce.
7. Return pork ribs onto the grill grate and then grill for 10 minutes until glazed.
8. When done, transfer ribs to a cutting board, let rest for 10 minutes, then cut it into slices and serve.

Nutrition Value:

- Calories: 250.8 Cal
- Fat: 16.3 g
- Carbs: 6.5 g
- Protein: 18.2 g
- Fiber: 0.2 g

Lemon Pepper Pork Tenderloin

Preparation time: 20 minutes
Cooking time: 20 minutes
Servings: 6

Ingredients:

- 2 pounds pork tenderloin, fat trimmed

For the Marinade:

- ½ teaspoon minced garlic
- 2 lemons, zested
- 1 teaspoon minced parsley
- 1/2 teaspoon salt
- 1/4 teaspoon ground black pepper
- 1 teaspoon lemon juice
- 2 tablespoons olive oil

Method:

1. Prepare the marinade and for this, take a small bowl, place all of its ingredients in it and whisk until combined.
2. Take a large plastic bag, pour marinade in it, add pork tenderloin, seal the bag, turn it upside down to coat the pork and let it marinate for a minimum of 2 hours in the refrigerator.
3. When ready to cook, switch on the Traeger grill, fill the grill hopper with apple-flavored wood pellets, power the grill on by using the control panel, select 'smoke' on the temperature dial, or set the temperature to 375 degrees F and let it preheat for a minimum of 15 minutes.
4. When the grill has preheated, open the lid, place pork tenderloin on the grill grate, shut the grill and smoke for 20 minutes until internal temperature reaches 145 degrees F, turning pork halfway.
5. When done, transfer pork to a cutting board, let it rest for 10 minutes, then cut it into slices and serve.

Nutrition Value:

- Calories: 288.5 Cal
- Fat: 16.6 g
- Carbs: 6.2 g
- Protein: 26.4 g
- Fiber: 1.2 g

Chinese BBQ Pork

Preparation time: 10 minutes
Cooking time: 2 hours
Servings: 8

Ingredients:

- 2 pork tenderloins, silver skin removed

For the Marinade:

- ½ teaspoon minced garlic
- 1 1/2 tablespoon brown sugar
- 1 teaspoon Chinese five-spice
- 1/4 cup honey
- 1 tablespoon Asian sesame oil
- 1/4 cup hoisin sauce
- 2 teaspoons red food coloring
- 1 tablespoon oyster sauce, optional
- 3 tablespoons soy sauce

For the Five-Spice Sauce:

- 1/4 teaspoon Chinese five-spice
- 3 tablespoons brown sugar
- 1 teaspoon yellow mustard
- 1/4 cup ketchup

Method:

1. Prepare the marinade and for this, take a small bowl, place all of its ingredients in it and whisk until combined.
2. Take a large plastic bag, pour marinade in it, add pork tenderloin, seal the bag, turn it upside down to coat the pork and let it marinate for a minimum of 8 hours in the refrigerator.
3. Switch on the Traeger grill, fill the grill hopper with maple-flavored wood pellets, power the grill on by using the control panel, select 'smoke' on the temperature

dial, or set the temperature to 225 degrees F and let it preheat for a minimum of 5 minutes.

4. Meanwhile, remove pork from the marinade, transfer marinade into a small saucepan, place it over medium-high heat and cook for 3 minutes, and then set aside until cooled.

5. When the grill has preheated, open the lid, place pork on the grill grate, shut the grill and smoke for 2 hours, basting with the marinade halfway.

6. Meanwhile, prepare the five-spice sauce and for this, take a small saucepan, place it over low heat, add all of its ingredients, stir until well combined and sugar has dissolved and cooked for 5 minutes until hot and thickened, set aside until required.

7. When done, transfer pork to a dish, let rest for 15 minutes, and meanwhile, change the smoking temperature of the grill to 450 degrees F and let it preheat for a minimum of 10 minutes.

8. Then return pork to the grill grate and cook for 3 minutes per side until slightly charred.

9. Transfer pork to a dish, let rest for 5 minutes, and then serve with prepared five-spice sauce.

Nutrition Value:

- Calories: 280 Cal
- Fat: 8 g
- Carbs: 12 g

- Protein: 40 g
- Fiber: 0 g

Smoked Sausages

Preparation time: 15 minutes
Cooking time: 3 hours
Servings: 4

Ingredients:

- 3 pounds ground pork
- 1 tablespoon onion powder
- 1 tablespoon garlic powder
- 1 teaspoon curing salt
- 4 teaspoon black pepper
- 1/2 tablespoon salt
- 1/2 tablespoon ground mustard
- Hog casings, soaked
- 1/2 cup ice water

Method:

1. Switch on the Traeger grill, fill the grill hopper with flavored wood pellets, power the grill on by using the control panel, select 'smoke' on the temperature dial, or set the temperature to 225 degrees F and let it preheat for a minimum of 15 minutes.
2. Meanwhile, take a medium bowl, place all the ingredients in it except for water and hog casings, and stir until well mixed.
3. Pour in water, stir until incorporated, place the mixture in a sausage stuffer, then stuff the hog casings and tie the link to the desired length.
4. When the grill has preheated, open the lid, place the sausage links on the grill grate, shut the grill, and smoke for 2 to 3 hours until the internal temperature reaches 155 degrees F.
5. When done, transfer sausages to a dish, let them rest for 5 minutes, then slice and serve.

Nutrition Value:

- Calories: 230 Cal
- Fat: 22 g
- Carbs: 2 g
- Protein: 14 g
- Fiber: 0 g

BBQ Baby Back Ribs

Preparation time: 15 minutes
Cooking time: 6 hours
Servings: 8

Ingredients:

- 2 racks of baby back pork ribs, membrane removed
- Pork and poultry rub as needed
- 1/2 cup brown sugar
- 1/3 cup honey, warmed
- 1/3 cup yellow mustard
- 1 tablespoon Worcestershire sauce
- 1 cup BBQ sauce
- 1/2 cup apple juice, divided

Method:

1. Switch on the Traeger grill, fill the grill hopper with hickory flavored wood pellets, power the grill on by using the control panel, select 'smoke' on the temperature dial, or set the temperature to 180 degrees F and let it preheat for a minimum of 15 minutes.
2. Meanwhile, take a small bowl, place mustard, and Worcestershire sauce in it, pour in ¼ cup apple juice and whisk until combined and smooth paste comes together.
3. Brush this paste on all sides of ribs and then season with pork and poultry rub until coated.
4. When the grill has preheated, open the lid, place ribs on the grill grate meat-side up, shut the grill and smoke for 3 hours.
5. After 3 hours, transfer ribs to a rimmed baking dish, let rest for 15 minutes, and meanwhile, change the smoking temperature of the grill to 225 degrees F and let it preheat for a minimum of 10 minutes.
6. Then return pork into the rimmed baking sheet to the grill grate and cook for 3 minutes per side until slightly charred.
7. When done, remove the baking sheet from the grill and work on one rib at a time, sprinkle half of the sugar over the rib, drizzle with half of the honey and half of the remaining apple juice, cover with aluminum foil to seal completely.

8. Repeat with the remaining ribs, return foiled ribs on the grill grate, shut with lid, and then smoke for 2 hours.
9. After 2 hours, uncover the grill, brush them with BBQ sauce generously, arrange them on the grill grate and grill for 1 hour until glazed.
10. When done, transfer ribs to a cutting board, let it rest for 15 minutes, slice into pieces and then serve.

Nutrition Value:

- Calories: 334 Cal
- Fat: 22.5 g
- Carbs: 6.5 g

- Protein: 24 g
- Fiber: 0.1 g

Roasted Whole Ham in Apricot Sauce

Preparation time: 15 minutes
Cooking time: 2 hours
Servings: 12

Ingredients:

- 8-pound whole ham, bone-in
- 16 ounces apricot BBQ sauce
- 2 tablespoon Dijon mustard
- 1/4 cup horseradish

Method:

1. Switch on the Traeger grill, fill the grill hopper with apple-flavored wood pellets, power the grill on by using the control panel, select 'smoke' on the temperature dial, or set the temperature to 325 degrees F and let it preheat for a minimum of 15 minutes.
2. Meanwhile, take a large roasting pan, line it with foil, and place ham on it.
3. When the grill has preheated, open the lid, place roasting pan containing ham on the grill grate, shut the grill and smoke for 1 hour and 30 minutes.
4. Meanwhile, prepare the glaze and for this, take a medium saucepan, place it over medium heat, add BBQ sauce, mustard, and horseradish, stir until mixed and cook for 5 minutes, set aside until required.
5. After 1 hour and 30 minutes smoking, brush ha generously with the prepared glaze and continue smoking for 30 minutes until internal temperature reaches 135 degrees F.
6. When done, remove roasting pan from the grill, let rest for 20 minutes and then cut into slices.
7. Serve ham with remaining glaze.

Nutrition Value:

- Calories: 157.7 Cal
- Fat: 5.6 g
- Carbs: 4.1 g
- Protein: 22.1 g
- Fiber: 0.1 g

Pork Belly

Preparation time: 10 minutes
Cooking time: 3 hours and 30 minutes
Servings: 8

Ingredients:

- 3 pounds pork belly, skin removed
- Pork and poultry rub as needed
- 4 tablespoons salt
- 1/2 teaspoon ground black pepper

Method:

1. Switch on the Traeger grill, fill the grill hopper with apple-flavored wood pellets, power the grill on by using the control panel, select 'smoke' on the temperature dial, or set the temperature to 275 degrees F and let it preheat for a minimum of 15 minutes.
2. Meanwhile, prepare the pork belly and for this, sprinkle pork and poultry rub, salt, and black pepper on all sides of pork belly until well coated.
3. When the grill has preheated, open the lid, place the pork belly on the grill grate, shut the grill and smoke for 3 hours and 30 minutes until the internal temperature reaches 200 degrees F.
4. When done, transfer pork belly to a cutting board, let it rest for 15 minutes, then cut it into slices and serve.

Nutrition Value:

- Calories: 430 Cal
- Fat: 44 g
- Carbs: 1 g
- Protein: 8 g
- Fiber: 0 g

Pulled Pork

Preparation time: 10 minutes
Cooking time: 9 hours
Servings: 12

Ingredients:

- 9 pounds pork shoulder, bone-in, fat trimmed
- Game rub as needed and more as required
- 2 cups apple cider

Method:

1. Switch on the Traeger grill, fill the grill hopper with apple-flavored wood pellets, power the grill on by using the control panel, select 'smoke' on the temperature dial, or set the temperature to 250 degrees F and let it preheat for a minimum of 15 minutes.
2. Meanwhile, prepare the pork shoulder, and for this, season it generously with game rub until well coated.
3. When the grill has preheated, open the lid, place pork should on the grill grate fat-side up, shut the grill and smoke for 5 hours, and then remove pork from the grill.
4. Take a large baking sheet, line it with 4 large aluminum foil pieces to wrap pork, place pork in the center, bring up the sides of the foil, pour in apple cider, and then wrap tightly.
5. Transfer baking sheet containing wrapped pork on the grill grate and then cook for 4 hours until the internal temperature reaches to 204 degrees F.
6. When done, remove the baking sheet from the grill, let it rest for 45 minutes, then uncover it, place the pork into a large dish and drain excess liquid into a bowl.
7. Shred pork by using two forks, remove and discard excess fat and bone, then drizzle with reserved liquid and season with some game rub.
8. Serve straight away.

Nutrition Value:

- Calories: 220.1 Cal
- Fat: 15 g
- Carbs: 1 g
- Protein: 20 g
- Fiber: 0 g

Pork Steak

Preparation time: 10 minutes
Cooking time: 20 minutes
Servings: 4

Ingredients:

For the Brine:

- 2-inch piece of orange peel
- 2 sprigs of thyme
- 4 tablespoons salt
- 4 black peppercorns
- 1 sprig of rosemary
- 2 tablespoons brown sugar
- 2 bay leaves
- 10 cups water

For Pork Steaks:

- 4 pork steaks, fat trimmed
- Game rub as needed

Method:

1. Prepare the brine and for this, take a large container, place all of its ingredients in it and stir until sugar has dissolved.
2. Place steaks in it, add some weights to keep steak submerge into the brine and let soak for 24 hours in the refrigerator.
3. When ready to cook, switch on the Traeger grill, fill the grill hopper with hickory flavored wood pellets, power the grill on by using the control panel, select 'smoke' on the temperature dial, or set the temperature to 225 degrees F and let it preheat for a minimum of 15 minutes.
4. Meanwhile, remove steaks from the brine, rinse well, pat dry with paper towels and then season well with game rub until coated.

5. When the grill has preheated, open the lid, place steaks on the grill grate, shut the grill and smoke for 10 minutes per side until the internal temperature reaches the 140 degrees F.
6. When done, transfer steaks to a cutting board, let them rest for 10 minutes, then cut into slices and serve.

Nutrition Value:

- Calories: 260 Cal
- Fat: 21 g
- Carbs: 1 g
- Protein: 17 g
- Fiber: 0 g

Chapter 6: Lamb Recipes

Roasted Leg of Lamb

Preparation time: 30 minutes
Cooking time: 2 hours
Servings: 12

Ingredients:

- 8 pounds leg of lamb, bone-in, fat trimmed
- 2 lemons, juiced, zested
- 1 tablespoon minced garlic
- 4 sprigs of rosemary, 1-inch diced
- 4 cloves of garlic, peeled, sliced lengthwise
- Salt as needed
- Ground black pepper as needed
- 2 teaspoons olive oil

Method:

1. Switch on the Traeger grill, fill the grill hopper with cherry flavored wood pellets, power the grill on by using the control panel, select 'smoke' on the temperature dial, or set the temperature to 450 degrees F and let it preheat for a minimum of 15 minutes.
2. Meanwhile, take a small bowl, place minced garlic in it, stir in oil and then rub this mixture on all sides of the lamb leg.
3. Then make ¾-inch deep cuts into the lamb meat, about two dozen, stuff each cut with garlic slices and rosemary, sprinkle with lemon zest, drizzle with lemon juice, and then season well with salt and black pepper.
4. When the grill has preheated, open the lid, place the leg of lamb on the grill grate, shut the grill, and smoke for 30 minutes.
5. Change the smoking temperature to 350 degrees F and then continue smoking for 1 hour and 30 minutes until the internal temperature reaches 130 degrees F.
6. When done, transfer lamb to a cutting board, let it rest for 15 minutes, then cut it into slices and serve.

Nutrition Value:

- Calories: 219 Cal
- Fat: 14 g
- Carbs: 1 g
- Protein: 22 g
- Fiber: 0 g

Greek-Style Roast Leg of Lamb

Preparation time: 25 minutes
Cooking time: 1 hour and 30 minutes
Servings: 12

Ingredients:

- 7 pounds leg of lamb, bone-in, fat trimmed
- 2 lemons, juiced
- 8 cloves of garlic, peeled, minced
- Salt as needed
- Ground black pepper as needed
- 1 teaspoon dried oregano
- 1 teaspoon dried rosemary
- 6 tablespoons olive oil

Method:

1. Make a small cut into the meat of lamb by using a paring knife, then stir together garlic, oregano, and rosemary and stuff this paste into the slits of the lamb meat.
2. Take a roasting pan, place lamb in it, then rub with lemon juice and olive oil, cover with a plastic wrap and let marinate for a minimum of 8 hours in the refrigerator.
3. When ready to cook, switch on the Traeger grill, fill the grill hopper with oak flavored wood pellets, power the grill on by using the control panel, select 'smoke' on the temperature dial, or set the temperature to 400 degrees F and let it preheat for a minimum of 15 minutes.
4. Meanwhile, remove the lamb from the refrigerator, bring it to room temperature, uncover it and then season well with salt and black pepper.
5. When the grill has preheated, open the lid, place food on the grill grate, shut the grill, and smoke for 30 minutes.
6. Change the smoking temperature to 350 degrees F and then continue smoking for 1 hour until the internal temperature reaches 140 degrees F.
7. When done, transfer lamb to a cutting board, let it rest for 15 minutes, then cut it into slices and serve.

Nutrition Value:

- Calories: 168 Cal
- Fat: 10 g
- Carbs: 2 g
- Protein: 17 g
- Fiber: 0.7 g

Lamb Chops

Preparation time: 10 minutes
Cooking time: 10 minutes
Servings: 8

Ingredients:

For the Lamb:

- 16 lamb chops, fat trimmed
- 2 tablespoons Greek Freak seasoning

For the Mint Sauce:

- 1 tablespoon chopped parsley
- 12 cloves of garlic, peeled
- 1 tablespoon chopped mint
- 1/4 teaspoon dried oregano
- 1 teaspoon salt
- 1/4 teaspoon ground black pepper
- 3/4 cup lemon juice
- 1 cup olive oil

Method:

1. Prepare the mint sauce and for this, place all of its ingredients in a food processor and then pulse for 1 minute until smooth.
2. Pour 1/3 cup of the mint sauce into a plastic bag, add lamb chops in it, seal the bag, turn it upside to coat lamb chops with the sauce and then let them marinate for a minimum of 30 minutes in the refrigerator.
3. When ready to cook, switch on the Traeger grill, fill the grill hopper with apple-flavored wood pellets, power the grill on by using the control panel, select 'smoke' on the temperature dial, or set the temperature to 450 degrees F and let it preheat for a minimum of 15 minutes.
4. Meanwhile, remove lamb chops from the marinade and then season with Greek seasoning.

5. When the grill has preheated, open the lid, place lamb chops on the grill grate, shut the grill and smoke for 4 to 5 minutes per side until cooked to the desired level.
6. When done, transfer lamb chops to a dish and then serve.

Nutrition Value:

- Calories: 362 Cal
- Fat: 26 g
- Carbs: 0 g
- Protein: 31 g
- Fiber: 0 g

Smoked Rack of Lamb

Preparation time: 10 minutes
Cooking time: 1 hour and 15 minutes
Servings: 4

Ingredients:

- 1 rack of lamb rib, membrane removed

For the Marinade:

- 1 lemon, juiced
- 2 teaspoons minced garlic
- 1 teaspoon salt
- 1 teaspoon ground black pepper
- 1 teaspoon dried thyme
- ¼ cup balsamic vinegar
- 1 teaspoon dried basil

For the Glaze:

- 2 tablespoons soy sauce
- ¼ cup Dijon mustard
- 2 tablespoons Worcestershire sauce
- ¼ cup red wine

Method:

1. Prepare the marinade and for this, take a small bowl, place all the ingredients in it and whisk until combined.
2. Place the rack of lamb into a large plastic bag, pour in marinade, seal the bag, turn it upside down to coat lamb with the marinade and let it marinate for a minimum of 8 hours in the refrigerator.
3. When ready to cook, switch on the Traeger grill, fill the grill hopper with flavored wood pellets, power the grill on by using the control panel, select 'smoke' on the temperature dial, or set the temperature to 300 degrees F and let it preheat for a minimum of 5 minutes.

4. Meanwhile, prepare the glaze and for this, take a small bowl, place all of its ingredients in it and whisk until combined.
5. When the grill has preheated, open the lid, place lamb rack on the grill grate, shut the grill and smoke for 15 minutes.
6. Brush with glaze, flip the lamb and then continue smoking for 1 hour and 15 minutes until the internal temperature reaches 145 degrees F, basting with the glaze every 30 minutes.
7. When done, transfer lamb rack to a cutting board, let it rest for 15 minutes, cut it into slices, and then serve.

Nutrition Value:

- Calories: 323 Cal
- Fat: 18 g
- Carbs: 13 g
- Protein: 25 g
- Fiber: 1 g

Rosemary Lamb

Preparation time: 10 minutes
Cooking time: 3 hours
Servings: 2

Ingredients:

- 1 rack of lamb rib, membrane removed
- 12 baby potatoes
- 1 bunch of asparagus, ends trimmed
- Ground black pepper, as needed
- Salt, as needed
- 1 teaspoon dried rosemary
- 2 tablespoons olive oil
- 1/2 cup butter, unsalted

Method:

1. Switch on the Traeger grill, fill the grill hopper with flavored wood pellets, power the grill on by using the control panel, select 'smoke' on the temperature dial, or set the temperature to 225 degrees F and let it preheat for a minimum of 5 minutes.
2. Meanwhile, drizzle oil on both sides of lamb ribs and then sprinkle with rosemary.
3. Take a deep baking dish, place potatoes in it, add butter and mix until coated.
4. When the grill has preheated, open the lid, place lamb ribs on the grill grate along with potatoes in the baking dish, shut the grill and smoke for 3 hours until the internal temperature reaches 145 degrees F.
5. Add asparagus into the baking dish in the last 20 minutes and, when done, remove baking dish from the grill and transfer lamb to a cutting board.
6. Let lamb rest for 15 minutes, cut it into slices, and then serve with potatoes and asparagus.

Nutrition Value:

- Calories: 355 Cal
- Fat: 12.5 g
- Carbs: 25 g
- Protein: 35 g
- Fiber: 6 g

Lamb Chops with Rosemary and Olive oil

Preparation time: 10 minutes
Cooking time: 50 minutes
Servings: 4

Ingredients:

- 12 Lamb loin chops, fat trimmed
- 1 tablespoon chopped rosemary leaves
- Salt as needed for dry brining
- Jeff's original rub as needed
- ¼ cup olive oil

Method:

1. Take a cookie sheet, place lamb chops on it, sprinkle with salt, and then refrigerate for 2 hours.
2. Meanwhile, take a small bowl, place rosemary leaves in it, stir in oil and let the mixture stand for 1 hour.
3. When ready to cook, switch on the Traeger grill, fill the grill hopper with apple-flavored wood pellets, power the grill on by using the control panel, select 'smoke' on the temperature dial, or set the temperature to 225 degrees F and let it preheat for a minimum of 5 minutes.
4. Meanwhile, brush rosemary-oil mixture on all sides of lamb chops and then sprinkle with Jeff's original rub.
5. When the grill has preheated, open the lid, place lamb chops on the grill grate, shut the grill and smoke for 50 minutes until the internal temperature of lamb chops reach to 138 degrees F.
6. When done, wrap lamb chops in foil, let them rest for 7 minutes and then serve.

Nutrition Value:

- Calories: 171.5 Cal
- Fat: 7.8 g
- Carbs: 0.4 g
- Protein: 23.2 g
- Fiber: 0.1 g

Boneless Leg of Lamb

Preparation time: 10 minutes
Cooking time: 4 hours
Servings: 4

Ingredients:

- 2 1/2 pounds leg of lamb, boneless, fat trimmed

For the Marinade:

- 2 teaspoons minced garlic
- 1 tablespoon ground black pepper
- 2 tablespoons salt
- 1 teaspoon thyme
- 2 tablespoons oregano
- 2 tablespoons olive oil

Method:

1. Take a small bowl, place all the ingredients for the marinade in it and then stir until combined.
2. Rub the marinade on all sides of lamb, then place it in a large sheet, cover with a plastic wrap and marinate for a minimum of 1 hour in the refrigerator.
3. When ready to cook, switch on the Traeger grill, fill the grill hopper with apple-flavored wood pellets, power the grill on by using the control panel, select 'smoke' on the temperature dial, or set the temperature to 250 degrees F and let it preheat for a minimum of 5 minutes.
4. Meanwhile,
5. When the grill has preheated, open the lid, place the lamb on the grill grate, shut the grill and smoke for 4 hours until the internal temperature reaches 145 degrees F.
6. When done, transfer lamb to a cutting board, let it stand for 10 minutes, then carve it into slices and serve.

Nutrition Value:

- Calories: 213 Cal
- Fat: 9 g
- Carbs: 1 g
- Protein: 29 g

- Fiber: 0 g

Smoked Lamb Shoulder

Preparation time: 10 minutes
Cooking time: 4 hours
Servings: 6

Ingredients:

- 8 pounds lamb shoulder, fat trimmed
- 2 tablespoons olive oil
- Salt as needed

For the Rub:

- 1 tablespoon dried oregano
- 2 tablespoons salt
- 1 tablespoon crushed dried bay leaf
- 1 tablespoon sugar
- 2 tablespoons dried crushed sage
- 1 tablespoon dried thyme
- 1 tablespoon ground black pepper
- 1 tablespoon dried basil
- 1 tablespoon dried rosemary
- 1 tablespoon dried parsley

Method:

1. Switch on the Traeger grill, fill the grill hopper with cherry flavored wood pellets, power the grill on by using the control panel, select 'smoke' on the temperature dial, or set the temperature to 250 degrees F and let it preheat for a minimum of 5 minutes.
2. Meanwhile, prepare the rub and for this, take a small bowl, place all of its ingredients in it and stir until mixed.
3. Brush lamb with oil and then sprinkle with prepared rub until evenly coated.
4. When the grill has preheated, open the lid, place lamb should on the grill grate fat-side up, shut the grill and smoke for 3 hours.
5. Then change the smoking temperature to 325 degrees F and continue smoking to 1 hour until fat renders, and the internal temperature reaches 195 degrees F.

6. When done, wrap lamb should in aluminum foil and let it rest for 20 minutes.
7. Pull lamb shoulder by using two forks and then serve.

Nutrition Value:

- Calories: 300 Cal
- Fat: 24 g
- Carbs: 0 g

- Protein: 19 g
- Fiber: 0 g

Herby Lamb Chops

Preparation time: 10 minutes
Cooking time: 2 hours
Servings: 4

Ingredients:

- 8 lamb chops, each about ¾-inch thick, fat trimmed

For the Marinade:

- 1 teaspoon minced garlic
- Salt as needed
- 1 tablespoon dried rosemary
- Ground black pepper as needed
- ½ tablespoon dried thyme
- 3 tablespoons balsamic vinegar
- 1 tablespoon Dijon mustard
- ½ cup olive oil

Method:

1. Prepare the marinade and for this, take a small bowl, place all of its ingredients in it and stir until well combined.
2. Place lamb chops in a large plastic bag, pour in marinade, seal the bag, turn it upside down to coat lamb chops with the marinade and let it marinate for a minimum of 4 hours in the refrigerator.
3. When ready to cook, switch on the Traeger grill, fill the grill hopper with flavored wood pellets, power the grill on by using the control panel, select 'smoke' on the temperature dial, or set the temperature to 450 degrees F and let it preheat for a minimum of 5 minutes.
4. Meanwhile, remove lamb chops from the refrigerator and bring them to room temperature.
5. When the grill has preheated, open the lid, place lamb chops on the grill grate, shut the grill and smoke for 5 minutes per side until seared.
6. When done, transfer lamb chops to a dish, let them rest for 5 minutes and then serve.

Nutrition Value:

- Calories: 280 Cal
- Fat: 12.3 g
- Carbs: 8.3 g
- Protein: 32.7 g
- Fiber: 1.2 g

Garlic Rack of Lamb

Preparation time: 10 minutes
Cooking time: 3 hours
Servings: 4

Ingredients:

- 1 rack of lamb, membrane removed

For the Marinade:

- 2 teaspoons minced garlic
- 1 teaspoon dried basil
- 1/3 cup cream sherry
- 1 teaspoon dried oregano
- 1/3 cup Marsala wine
- 1 teaspoon dried rosemary
- ½ teaspoon ground black pepper
- 1/3 cup balsamic vinegar
- 2 tablespoons olive oil

Method:

1. Prepare the marinade and for this, take a small bowl, place all of its ingredients in it and stir until well combined.
2. Place lamb rack in a large plastic bag, pour in marinade, seal the bag, turn it upside down to coat lamb with the marinade and let it marinate for a minimum of 45 minutes in the refrigerator.
3. When ready to cook, switch on the Traeger grill, fill the grill hopper with flavored wood pellets, power the grill on by using the control panel, select 'smoke' on the temperature dial, or set the temperature to 250 degrees F and let it preheat for a minimum of 5 minutes.
4. Meanwhile,
5. When the grill has preheated, open the lid, place lamb rack on the grill grate, shut the grill, and smoke for 3 hours until the internal temperature reaches 165 degrees F.

6. When done, transfer lamb rack to a cutting board, let it rest for 10 minutes, then cut into slices and serve.

Nutrition Value:

- Calories: 210 Cal
- Fat: 11 g
- Carbs: 3 g

- Protein: 25 g
- Fiber: 1 g

Chapter 7: Poultry Recipes

Herb Roasted Turkey

Preparation time: 15 minutes
Cooking time: 3 hours and 30 minutes
Servings: 12

Ingredients:

- 14 pounds turkey, cleaned
- 2 tablespoons chopped mixed herbs
- Pork and poultry rub as needed
- 1/4 teaspoon ground black pepper
- 3 tablespoons butter, unsalted, melted
- 8 tablespoons butter, unsalted, softened
- 2 cups chicken broth

Method:

1. Clean the turkey by removing the giblets, wash it inside out, pat dry with paper towels, then place it on a roasting pan and tuck the turkey wings by tiring with butcher's string.
2. Switch on the Traeger grill, fill the grill hopper with hickory flavored wood pellets, power the grill on by using the control panel, select 'smoke' on the temperature dial, or set the temperature to 325 degrees F and let it preheat for a minimum of 15 minutes.
3. Meanwhile, prepared herb butter and for this, take a small bowl, place the softened butter in it, add black pepper and mixed herbs and beat until fluffy.
4. Place some of the prepared herb butter underneath the skin of turkey by using a handle of a wooden spoon, and massage the skin to distribute butter evenly.
5. Then rub the exterior of the turkey with melted butter, season with pork and poultry rub, and pour the broth in the roasting pan.
6. When the grill has preheated, open the lid, place roasting pan containing turkey on the grill grate, shut the grill and smoke for 3 hours and 30 minutes until the internal temperature reaches 165 degrees F and the top has turned golden brown.

7. When done, transfer turkey to a cutting board, let it rest for 30 minutes, then carve it into slices and serve.

Nutrition Value:

- Calories: 154.6 Cal
- Fat: 3.1 g
- Carbs: 8.4 g
- Protein: 28.8 g
- Fiber: 0.4 g

Turkey Legs

Preparation time: 24 hours
Cooking time: 5 hours
Servings: 4

Ingredients:

- 4 turkey legs

For the Brine:

- 1/2 cup curing salt
- 1 tablespoon whole black peppercorns
- 1 cup BBQ rub
- 1/2 cup brown sugar
- 2 bay leaves
- 2 teaspoons liquid smoke
- 16 cups of warm water
- 4 cups ice
- 8 cups of cold water

Method:

1. Prepare the brine and for this, take a large stockpot, place it over high heat, pour warm water in it, add peppercorn, bay leaves, and liquid smoke, stir in salt, sugar, and BBQ rub and bring it to a boil.
2. Remove pot from heat, bring it to room temperature, then pour in cold water, add ice cubes and let the brine chill in the refrigerator.
3. Then add turkey legs in it, submerge them completely, and let soak for 24 hours in the refrigerator.
4. After 24 hours, remove turkey legs from the brine, rinse well and pat dry with paper towels.
5. When ready to cook, switch on the Traeger grill, fill the grill hopper with hickory flavored wood pellets, power the grill on by using the control panel, select 'smoke' on the temperature dial, or set the temperature to 250 degrees F and let it preheat for a minimum of 15 minutes.

6. When the grill has preheated, open the lid, place turkey legs on the grill grate, shut the grill, and smoke for 5 hours until nicely browned and the internal temperature reaches 165 degrees F.
7. Serve immediately.

Nutrition Value:

- Calories: 416 Cal
- Fat: 13.3 g
- Carbs: 0 g
- Protein: 69.8 g
- Fiber: 0 g

Turkey Breast

Preparation time: 12 hours
Cooking time: 8 hours
Servings: 6

Ingredients:

For the Brine:

- 2 pounds turkey breast, deboned
- 2 tablespoons ground black pepper
- 1/4 cup salt
- 1 cup brown sugar
- 4 cups cold water

For the BBQ Rub:

- 2 tablespoons dried onions
- 2 tablespoons garlic powder
- 1/4 cup paprika
- 2 tablespoons ground black pepper
- 1 tablespoon salt
- 2 tablespoons brown sugar
- 2 tablespoons red chili powder
- 1 tablespoon cayenne pepper
- 2 tablespoons sugar
- 2 tablespoons ground cumin

Method:

1. Prepare the brine and for this, take a large bowl, add salt, black pepper, and sugar in it, pour in water, and stir until sugar has dissolved.
2. Place turkey breast in it, submerge it completely and let it soak for a minimum of 12 hours in the refrigerator.
3. Meanwhile, prepare the BBQ rub and for this, take a small bowl, place all of its ingredients in it and then stir until combined, set aside until required.

4. Then remove turkey breast from the brine and season well with the prepared BBQ rub.
5. When ready to cook, switch on the Traeger grill, fill the grill hopper with apple-flavored wood pellets, power the grill on by using the control panel, select 'smoke' on the temperature dial, or set the temperature to 180 degrees F and let it preheat for a minimum of 15 minutes.
6. When the grill has preheated, open the lid, place turkey breast on the grill grate, shut the grill, change the smoking temperature to 225 degrees F, and smoke for 8 hours until the internal temperature reaches 160 degrees F.
7. When done, transfer turkey to a cutting board, let it rest for 10 minutes, then cut it into slices and serve.

Nutrition Value:

- Calories: 250 Cal
- Fat: 5 g
- Carbs: 31 g
- Protein: 18 g
- Fiber: 5 g

HellFire Chicken Wings

Preparation time: 15 minutes
Cooking time: 40 minutes
Servings: 6

Ingredients:

- 3 pounds chicken wings, tips removed
- 2 tablespoons olive oil

For the Rub:

- 1 teaspoon onion powder
- 1 teaspoon salt
- 1 teaspoon garlic powder
- 1 tablespoon paprika
- 1 teaspoon ground black pepper
- 1 teaspoon celery seed
- 1 teaspoon cayenne pepper
- 2 teaspoons brown sugar

For the Sauce:

- 4 jalapeno peppers, sliced crosswise
- 8 tablespoons butter, unsalted
- 1/2 cup hot sauce
- 1/2 cup cilantro leaves

Method:

1. Switch on the Traeger grill, fill the grill hopper with hickory flavored wood pellets, power the grill on by using the control panel, select 'smoke' on the temperature dial, or set the temperature to 350 degrees F and let it preheat for a minimum of 15 minutes.
2. Prepare the chicken wings and for this, remove tips from the wings, cut each chicken wing through the joint into two pieces, and then place in a large bowl.

3. Prepare the rub and for this, take a small bowl, place all of its ingredients in it and then stir until combined.
4. Sprinkle prepared rub on the chicken wings and then toss until well coated.
5. Meanwhile,
6. When the grill has preheated, open the lid, place chicken wings on the grill grate, shut the grill and smoke for 40 minutes until golden brown and skin have turned crisp, turning halfway.
7. Meanwhile, prepare the sauce and for this, take a small saucepan, place it over medium-low heat, add butter in it and when it melts, add jalapeno and cook for 4 minutes.
8. Then stir in hot sauce and cilantro until mixed and remove the pan from heat.
9. When done, transfer chicken wings to a dish, top with prepared sauce, toss until coated, and then serve.

Nutrition Value:

- Calories: 250 Cal
- Fat: 15 g
- Carbs: 11 g
- Protein: 19 g
- Fiber: 1 g

Spicy BBQ Chicken

Preparation time: 8 hours and 10 minutes
Cooking time: 3 hours
Servings: 6

Ingredients:

- 1 whole chicken, cleaned

For the Marinade:

- 1 medium white onion, peeled
- 6 Thai chilies
- 5 cloves of garlic, peeled
- 1 scotch bonnet
- 3 tablespoons salt
- 2 tablespoons sugar
- 2 tablespoons sweet paprika
- 4 cups grapeseed oil

Method:

1. Prepare the marinade, and for this, place all of its ingredients in a food processor and pulse for 2 minutes until smooth.
2. Smoother whole chicken with the prepared marinade and let it marinate in the refrigerator for a minimum of 8 hours.
3. When ready to cook, switch on the Traeger grill, fill the grill hopper with apple-flavored wood pellets, power the grill on by using the control panel, select 'smoke' on the temperature dial, or set the temperature to 300 degrees F and let it preheat for a minimum of 15 minutes.
4. When the grill has preheated, open the lid, place chicken on the grill grate breast-side up, shut the grill and smoke for 3 hours until the internal temperature of chicken reaches 165 degrees F.
5. When done, transfer chicken to a cutting board, let it rest for 15 minutes, then cut into slices and serve.

Nutrition Value:

- Calories: 100 Cal
- Fat: 2.8 g
- Carbs: 13 g
- Protein: 3.5 g
- Fiber: 2 g

BBQ Half Chickens

Preparation time: 15 minutes
Cooking time: 75 minutes
Servings: 4

Ingredients:

- 3.5-pound whole chicken, cleaned, halved
- Summer rub as needed
- Apricot BBQ sauce as needed

Method:

1. Switch on the Traeger grill, fill the grill hopper with apple-flavored wood pellets, power the grill on by using the control panel, select 'smoke' on the temperature dial, or set the temperature to 375 degrees F and let it preheat for a minimum of 15 minutes.
2. Meanwhile, cut chicken in half along with backbone and then season with summer rub.
3. When the grill has preheated, open the lid, place chicken halves on the grill grate skin-side up, shut the grill, change the smoking temperature to 225 degrees F, and smoke for 1 hour and 30 minutes until the internal temperature reaches 160 degrees F.
4. Then brush chicken generously with apricot sauce and continue grilling for 10 minutes until glazed.
5. When done, transfer chicken to cutting to a dish, let it rest for 5 minutes, and then serve.

Nutrition Value:

- Calories: 435 Cal
- Fat: 20 g
- Carbs: 20 g
- Protein: 42 g
- Fiber: 1 g

Teriyaki Wings

Preparation time: 8 hours
Cooking time: 50 minutes
Servings: 8

Ingredients:

- 2 ½ pounds large chicken wings
- 1 tablespoon toasted sesame seeds

For the Marinade:

- 2 scallions, sliced
- 2 tablespoons grated ginger
- ½ teaspoon minced garlic
- 1/4 cup brown sugar
- 1/2 cup soy sauce
- 2 tablespoon rice wine vinegar
- 2 teaspoons sesame oil
- 1/4 cup water

Method:

1. Prepare the chicken wings and for this, remove tips from the wings, cut each chicken wing through the joint into three pieces, and then place in a large plastic bag.
2. Prepare the sauce and for this, take a small saucepan, place it over medium-high heat, add all of its ingredients in it, stir until mixed, and bring it to a boil.
3. Then switch heat to medium level, simmer the sauce for 10 minutes, and when done, cool the sauce completely.
4. Pour the sauce over chicken wings, seal the bag, turn it upside down to coat chicken wings with the sauce and let it marinate for a minimum of 8 hours in the refrigerator.
5. When ready to cook, switch on the Traeger grill, fill the grill hopper with maple-flavored wood pellets, power the grill on by using the control panel, select 'smoke' on the temperature dial, or set the temperature to 350 degrees F and let it preheat for a minimum of 15 minutes.

6. Meanwhile,
7. When the grill has preheated, open the lid, place chicken wings on the grill grate, shut the grill and smoke for 50 minutes until crispy and meat is no longer pink, turning halfway.
8. When done, transfer chicken wings to a dish, sprinkle with sesame seeds and then serve.

Nutrition Value:

- Calories: 150 Cal
- Fat: 7.5 g
- Carbs: 6 g
- Protein: 12 g
- Fiber: 1 g

Korean Chicken Wings

Preparation time: 4 hours
Cooking time: 1 hour
Servings: 6

Ingredients:

- 3 pounds of chicken wings
- 2 tablespoons olive oil

For the Brine:

- 1 head garlic, halved
- 1 lemon, halved
- 1/2 cup sugar
- 1 cup of sea salt
- 4 sprigs of thyme
- 10 peppercorns
- 16 cups of water

For the Sauce:

- 2 teaspoons minced garlic
- 1/2 cup gochujang hot pepper paste
- 1 tablespoon grated ginger
- 2 tablespoons of rice wine vinegar
- 1/3 cup honey
- 1/4 cup soy sauce
- 2 tablespoons lime juice
- 2 tablespoons toasted sesame oil
- 1/4 cup melted butter

Method:

1. Prepare the brine and for this, take a large stockpot, place it over high heat, pour in water, stir in salt and sugar until dissolved, and bring to a boil.

2. Then remove the pot from heat, add remaining ingredients for the brine, and bring the brine to room temperature.
3. Add chicken wings, submerge them completely, cover the pot and let wings soak for a minimum of 4 hours in the refrigerator.
4. When ready to cook, switch on the Traeger grill, fill the grill hopper with flavored wood pellets, power the grill on by using the control panel, select 'smoke' on the temperature dial, or set the temperature to 375 degrees F and let it preheat for a minimum of 15 minutes.
5. Meanwhile, remove chicken wings from the brine, pat dry with paper towels, place them in a large bowl, drizzle with oil and toss until well coated.
6. When the grill has preheated, open the lid, place chicken wings on the grill grate, shut the grill, and smoke for 1 hour until the internal temperature reaches 165 degrees F.
7. Meanwhile, prepare the sauce and for this, take a medium bowl, place all of the sauce ingredients in it and whisk until smooth.
8. When done, transfer chicken wings to a dish, top with prepared sauce, toss until coated, and then serve.

Nutrition Value:

- Calories: 137 Cal
- Fat: 9 g
- Carbs: 4 g
- Protein: 8 g
- Fiber: 1 g

Garlic Parmesan Chicken Wings

Preparation time: 15 minutes
Cooking time: 20 minutes
Servings: 6

Ingredients:

- 5 pounds of chicken wings
- 1/2 cup chicken rub
- 3 tablespoons chopped parsley
- 1 cup shredded parmesan cheese

For the Sauce:

- 5 teaspoons minced garlic
- 2 tablespoons chicken rub
- 1 cup butter, unsalted

Method:

1. Switch on the Traeger grill, fill the grill hopper with cherry flavored wood pellets, power the grill on by using the control panel, select 'smoke' on the temperature dial, or set the temperature to 450 degrees F and let it preheat for a minimum of 15 minutes.
2. Meanwhile, take a large bowl, place chicken wings in it, sprinkle with chicken rub and toss until well coated.
3. When the grill has preheated, open the lid, place chicken wings on the grill grate, shut the grill, and smoke for 10 minutes per side until the internal temperature reaches 165 degrees F.
4. Meanwhile, prepare the sauce and for this, take a medium saucepan, place it over medium heat, add all the ingredients for the sauce in it and cook for 10 minutes until smooth, set aside until required.
5. When done, transfer chicken wings to a dish, top with prepared sauce, toss until mixed, garnish with cheese and parsley and then serve.

Nutrition Value:

- Calories: 180 Cal
- Fat: 1 g
- Carbs: 8 g
- Protein: 0 g
- Fiber: 0 g

Rosemary Orange Chicken

Preparation time: 2 hours
Cooking time: 45 minutes
Servings: 6

Ingredients:

- 4 pounds chicken, backbone removed

For the Marinade:

- 2 teaspoons salt
- 3 tablespoons chopped rosemary leaves
- 2 teaspoons Dijon mustard
- 1 orange, zested
- 1/4 cup olive oil
- ¼ cup of orange juice

Method:

1. Prepare the chicken and for this, rinse the chicken, pat dry with paper towels and then place in a large baking dish.
2. Prepare the marinade and for this, take a medium bowl, place all of its ingredients in it and whisk until combined.
3. Cover chicken with the prepared marinade, cover with a plastic wrap, and then marinate for a minimum of 2 hours in the refrigerator, turning halfway.
4. When ready to cook, switch on the Traeger grill, fill the grill hopper with flavored wood pellets, power the grill on by using the control panel, select 'smoke' on the temperature dial, or set the temperature to 350 degrees F and let it preheat for a minimum of 5 minutes.
5. When the grill has preheated, open the lid, place chicken on the grill grate skin-side down, shut the grill and smoke for 45 minutes until well browned, and the internal temperature reaches 165 degrees F.
6. When done, transfer chicken to a cutting board, let it rest for 10 minutes, cut it into slices, and then serve.

Nutrition Value:

- Calories: 258 Cal
- Fat: 17.4 g
- Carbs: 5.2 g
- Protein: 19.3 g
- Fiber: 0.3 g

Chapter 8: Fish and Seafood Recipes

Jerk Shrimp

Preparation time: 15 minutes
Cooking time: 6
Servings: 12

Ingredients:

- 2 pounds shrimp, peeled, deveined
- 3 tablespoons olive oil

For the Spice Mix:

- 1 teaspoon garlic powder
- 1 teaspoon of sea salt
- 1/4 teaspoon ground cayenne
- 1 tablespoon brown sugar
- 1/8 teaspoon smoked paprika
- 1 tablespoon smoked paprika
- 1/4 teaspoon ground thyme
- 1 lime, zested

Method:

1. Switch on the Traeger grill, fill the grill hopper with flavored wood pellets, power the grill on by using the control panel, select 'smoke' on the temperature dial, or set the temperature to 450 degrees F and let it preheat for a minimum of 5 minutes.
2. Meanwhile, prepare the spice mix and for this, take a small bowl, place all of its ingredients in it and stir until mixed.
3. Take a large bowl, place shrimps in it, sprinkle with prepared spice mix, drizzle with oil and toss until well coated.
4. When the grill has preheated, open the lid, place shrimps on the grill grate, shut the grill and smoke for 3 minutes per side until firm and thoroughly cooked.
5. When done, transfer shrimps to a dish and then serve.

Nutrition Value:

- Calories: 131 Cal
- Fat: 4.3 g
- Carbs: 0 g
- Protein: 22 g
- Fiber: 0 g

Spicy Shrimps Skewers

Preparation time: 10 minutes
Cooking time: 6 minutes
Servings: 4

Ingredients:

- 2 pounds shrimp, peeled, and deveined

For the Marinade:

- 6 ounces Thai chilies
- 6 cloves of garlic, peeled
- 1 ½ teaspoon sugar
- 2 tablespoons Napa Valley rub
- 1 ½ tablespoon white vinegar
- 3 tablespoons olive oil

Method:

1. Prepare the marinade and for this, place all of its ingredients in a food processor and then pulse for 1 minute until smooth.
2. Take a large bowl, place shrimps on it, add prepared marinade, toss until well coated, and let marinate for a minimum of 30 minutes in the refrigerator.
3. When ready to cook, switch on the Traeger grill, fill the grill hopper with apple-flavored wood pellets, power the grill on by using the control panel, select 'smoke' on the temperature dial, or set the temperature to 450 degrees F and let it preheat for a minimum of 5 minutes.
4. Meanwhile, remove shrimps from the marinade and then thread onto skewers.
5. When the grill has preheated, open the lid, place shrimps' skewers on the grill grate, shut the grill and smoke for 3 minutes per side until firm.
6. When done, transfer shrimps' skewers to a dish and then serve.

Nutrition Value:

- Calories: 187.2 Cal
- Fat: 2.7 g
- Carbs: 2.7 g
- Protein: 23.2 g
- Fiber: 0.2 g

Lobster Tails

Preparation time: 10 minutes
Cooking time: 35 minutes
Servings: 4

Ingredients:

- 2 lobster tails, each about 10 ounces

For the Sauce:

- 2 tablespoons chopped parsley
- 1/4 teaspoon garlic salt
- 1 teaspoon paprika
- 1/4 teaspoon ground black pepper
- 1/4 teaspoon old bay seasoning
- 8 tablespoons butter, unsalted
- 2 tablespoons lemon juice

Method:

1. Switch on the Traeger grill, fill the grill hopper with flavored wood pellets, power the grill on by using the control panel, select 'smoke' on the temperature dial, or set the temperature to 450 degrees F and let it preheat for a minimum of 15 minutes.
2. Meanwhile, prepare the sauce and for this, take a small saucepan, place it over medium-low heat, add butter in it and when it melts, add remaining ingredients for the sauce and stir until combined, set aside until required.
3. Prepare the lobster and for this, cut the shell from the middle to the tail by using kitchen shears and then take the meat from the shell, keeping it attached at the base of the crab tail.
4. Then butterfly the crab meat by making a slit down the middle, then place lobster tails on a baking sheet and pour 1 tablespoon of sauce over each lobster tail, reserve the remaining sauce.
5. When the grill has preheated, open the lid, place crab tails on the grill grate, shut the grill and smoke for 30 minutes until opaque.
6. When done, transfer lobster tails to a dish and then serve with the remaining sauce.

Nutrition Value:

- Calories: 290 Cal
- Fat: 22 g
- Carbs: 1 g

- Protein: 20 g
- Fiber: 0.3 g

Lemon Garlic Scallops

Preparation time: 10 minutes
Cooking time: 5 minutes
Servings: 6

Ingredients:

- 1 dozen scallops
- 2 tablespoons chopped parsley
- Salt as needed
- 1 tablespoon olive oil
- 1 tablespoon butter, unsalted
- 1 teaspoon lemon zest

For the Garlic Butter:

- ½ teaspoon minced garlic
- 1 lemon, juiced
- 4 tablespoons butter, unsalted, melted

Method:

1. Switch on the Traeger grill, fill the grill hopper with alder flavored wood pellets, power the grill on by using the control panel, select 'smoke' on the temperature dial, or set the temperature to 400 degrees F and let it preheat for a minimum of 15 minutes.
2. Meanwhile, remove frill from scallops, pat dry with paper towels and then season with salt and black pepper.
3. When the grill has preheated, open the lid, place a skillet on the grill grate, add butter and oil, and when the butter melts, place seasoned scallops on it and then cook for 2 minutes until seared.
4. Meanwhile, prepare the garlic butter and for this, take a small bowl, place all of its ingredients in it and then whisk until combined.
5. Flip the scallops, top with some of the prepared garlic butter, and cook for another minute.
6. When done, transfer scallops to a dish, top with remaining garlic butter, sprinkle with parsley and lemon zest, and then serve.

Nutrition Value:

- Calories: 184 Cal
- Fat: 10 g
- Carbs: 1 g

- Protein: 22 g
- Fiber: 0.2 g

Halibut in Parchment

Preparation time: 15 minutes
Cooking time: 15 minutes
Servings: 4

Ingredients:

- 16 asparagus spears, trimmed, sliced into 1/2-inch pieces
- 2 ears of corn kernels
- 4 ounces halibut fillets, pin bones removed
- 2 lemons, cut into 12 slices
- Salt as needed
- Ground black pepper as needed
- 2 tablespoons olive oil
- 2 tablespoons chopped parsley

Method:

1. Switch on the Traeger grill, fill the grill hopper with flavored wood pellets, power the grill on by using the control panel, select 'smoke' on the temperature dial, or set the temperature to 450 degrees F and let it preheat for a minimum of 5 minutes.
2. Meanwhile, cut out 18-inch long parchment paper, place a fillet in the center of each parchment, season with salt and black pepper, and then drizzle with oil.
3. Cover each fillet with three lemon slices, overlapping slightly, sprinkle one-fourth of asparagus and corn on each fillet, season with some salt and black pepper, and seal the fillets and vegetables tightly to prevent steam from escaping the packet.
4. When the grill has preheated, open the lid, place fillet packets on the grill grate, shut the grill and smoke for 15 minutes until packets have turned slightly brown and puffed up.
5. When done, transfer packets to a dish, let them stand for 5 minutes, then cut 'X' in the center of each packet, carefully uncover the fillets an vegetables, sprinkle with parsley, and then serve.

Nutrition Value:

- Calories: 186.6 Cal
- Fat: 2.8 g
- Carbs: 14.2 g
- Protein: 25.7 g
- Fiber: 4.1 g

Chilean Sea Bass

Preparation time: 30 minutes
Cooking time: 40 minutes
Servings: 6

Ingredients:

- 4 sea bass fillets, skinless, each about 6 ounces
- Chicken rub as needed
- 8 tablespoons butter, unsalted
- 2 tablespoons chopped thyme leaves
- Lemon slices for serving

For the Marinade:

- 1 lemon, juiced
- 4 teaspoons minced garlic
- 1 tablespoon chopped thyme
- 1 teaspoon blackened rub
- 1 tablespoon chopped oregano
- 1/4 cup oil

Method:

1. Prepare the marinade and for this, take a small bowl, place all of its ingredients in it, stir until well combined, and then pour the mixture into a large plastic bag.
2. Add fillets in the bag, seal it, turn it upside down to coat fillets with the marinade and let it marinate for a minimum of 30 minutes in the refrigerator.
3. When ready to cook, switch on the Traeger grill, fill the grill hopper with apple-flavored wood pellets, power the grill on by using the control panel, select 'smoke' on the temperature dial, or set the temperature to 325 degrees F and let it preheat for a minimum of 15 minutes.
4. Meanwhile, take a large baking pan and place butter on it.
5. When the grill has preheated, open the lid, place baking pan on the grill grate, and wait until butter melts.
6. Remove fillets from the marinade, pour marinade into the pan with melted butter, then season fillets with chicken rubs until coated on all sides, then place them into

the pan, shut the grill and cook for 30 minutes until internal temperature reaches 160 degrees F, frequently basting with the butter sauce.

7. When done, transfer fillets to a dish, sprinkle with thyme and then serve with lemon slices.

Nutrition Value:

- Calories: 232 Cal
- Fat: 12.2 g
- Carbs: 0.8 g

- Protein: 28.2 g
- Fiber: 0.1 g

Sriracha Salmon

Preparation time: 2 hours and 10 minutes
Cooking time: 25 minutes
Servings: 4

Ingredients:

- 3-pound salmon, skin on

For the Marinade:

- 1 teaspoon lime zest
- 1 tablespoon minced garlic
- 1 tablespoon grated ginger
- Sea salt as needed
- Ground black pepper as needed
- 1/4 cup maple syrup
- 2 tablespoons soy sauce
- 2 tablespoons Sriracha sauce
- 1 tablespoon toasted sesame oil
- 1 tablespoon rice vinegar
- 1 teaspoon toasted sesame seeds

Method:

1. Prepare the marinade and for this, take a small bowl, place all of its ingredients in it, stir until well combined, and then pour the mixture into a large plastic bag.
2. Add salmon in the bag, seal it, turn it upside down to coat salmon with the marinade and let it marinate for a minimum of 2 hours in the refrigerator.
3. When ready to cook, switch on the Traeger grill, fill the grill hopper with flavored wood pellets, power the grill on by using the control panel, select 'smoke' on the temperature dial, or set the temperature to 450 degrees F and let it preheat for a minimum of 5 minutes.
4. Meanwhile, take a large baking sheet, line it with parchment paper, place salmon on its skin-side down and then brush with the marinade.
5. When the grill has preheated, open the lid, place baking sheet containing salmon on the grill grate, shut the grill and smoke for 25 minutes until thoroughly cooked.

6. When done, transfer salmon to a dish and then serve.

Nutrition Value:

- Calories: 360 Cal
- Fat: 21 g
- Carbs: 28 g

- Protein: 16 g
- Fiber: 1.5 g

Grilled Rainbow Trout

Preparation time: 1 hour
Cooking time: 2 hours
Servings: 6

Ingredients:

- 6 rainbow trout, cleaned, butterfly

For the Brine:

- 1/4 cup salt
- 1 tablespoon ground black pepper
- 1/2 cup brown sugar
- 2 tablespoons soy sauce
- 16 cups water

Method:

1. Prepare the brine and for this, take a large container, add all of its ingredients in it, stir until sugar has dissolved, then add trout and let soak for 1 hour in the refrigerator.
2. When ready to cook, switch on the Traeger grill, fill the grill hopper with oak flavored wood pellets, power the grill on by using the control panel, select 'smoke' on the temperature dial, or set the temperature to 225 degrees F and let it preheat for a minimum of 15 minutes.
3. Meanwhile, remove trout from the brine and pat dry with paper towels.
4. When the grill has preheated, open the lid, place trout on the grill grate, shut the grill and smoke for 2 hours until thoroughly cooked and tender.
5. When done, transfer trout to a dish and then serve.

Nutrition Value:

- Calories: 250 Cal
- Fat: 12 g
- Carbs: 1.4 g
- Protein: 33 g
- Fiber: 0.3 g

Cider Salmon

Preparation time: 9 hours
Cooking time: 1 hour
Servings: 4

Ingredients:

- 1 ½ pound salmon fillet, skin-on, center-cut, pin bone removed

For the Brine:

- 4 juniper berries, crushed
- 1 bay leaf, crumbled
- 1-piece star anise, broken
- 1 1/2 cups apple cider

For the Cure:

- 1/2 cup salt
- 1 teaspoon ground black pepper
- 1/4 cup brown sugar
- 2 teaspoons barbecue rub

Method:

1. Prepare the brine and for this, take a large container, add all of its ingredients in it, stir until mixed, then add salmon and let soak for a minimum of 8 hours in the refrigerator.
2. Meanwhile, prepare the cure and for this, take a small bowl, place all of its ingredients in it and stir until combined.
3. After 8 hours, remove salmon from the brine, then take a baking dish, place half of the cure in it, top with salmon skin-side down, sprinkle remaining cure on top, cover with plastic wrap and let it rest for 1 hour in the refrigerator.
4. When ready to cook, switch on the Traeger grill, fill the grill hopper with oak flavored wood pellets, power the grill on by using the control panel, select 'smoke' on the temperature dial, or set the temperature to 200 degrees F and let it preheat for a minimum of 5 minutes.

5. Meanwhile, remove salmon from the cure, pat dry with paper towels, and then sprinkle with black pepper.
6. When the grill has preheated, open the lid, place salmon on the grill grate, shut the grill, and smoke for 1 hour until the internal temperature reaches 150 degrees F.
7. When done, transfer salmon to a cutting board, let it rest for 5 minutes, then remove the skin and serve.

Nutrition Value:

- Calories: 233 Cal
- Fat: 14 g
- Carbs: 0 g
- Protein: 25 g
- Fiber: 0 g

Cajun Shrimp

Preparation time: 4 hours
Cooking time: 8 minutes
Servings: 6

Ingredients:

- 2 pounds shrimp, peeled, deveined

For the Marinade:

- 1 teaspoon minced garlic
- 1 lemon, juiced
- 1 teaspoon salt
- 1 tablespoon Cajun shake
- 4 tablespoons olive oil

Method:

1. Prepare the marinade and for this, take a small bowl, place all of its ingredients in it, stir until well combined, and then pour the mixture into a large plastic bag.
2. Add shrimps in the bag, seal it, turn it upside down to coat salmon with the marinade and let it marinate for a minimum of 4 hours in the refrigerator.
3. When ready to cook, Switch on the Traeger grill, fill the grill hopper with flavored wood pellets, power the grill on by using the control panel, select 'smoke' on the temperature dial, or set the temperature to 450 degrees F and let it preheat for a minimum of 5 minutes.
4. Meanwhile,
5. When the grill has preheated, open the lid, place shrimps on the grill grate, shut the grill and smoke for 4 minutes per side until firm.
6. When done, transfer shrimps to a dish and then serve.

Nutrition Value:

- Calories: 92 Cal
- Fat: 7.6 g
- Carbs: 2.2 g
- Protein: 4.6 g
- Fiber: 0.8 g

Chapter 9: Game Recipes

Cornish Game Hens

Preparation time: 10 minutes
Cooking time: 1 hour
Servings: 6

Ingredients:

- 4 Cornish game hens, giblets removed
- 4 teaspoons chicken rub
- 4 sprigs of rosemary
- 4 tablespoons butter, unsalted, melted

Method:

1. Switch on the Traeger grill, fill the grill hopper with mesquite flavored wood pellets, power the grill on by using the control panel, select 'smoke' on the temperature dial, or set the temperature to 375 degrees F and let it preheat for a minimum of 15 minutes.
2. Meanwhile, rinse the hens, pat dry with paper towels, tie the wings by using a butcher's strong, then rub evenly with melted butter, sprinkle with chicken rub and stuff cavity of each hen with a rosemary sprig.
3. When the grill has preheated, open the lid, place hens on the grill grate, shut the grill, and smoke for 1 hour until thoroughly cooked and internal temperature reaches 165 degrees F.
4. When done, transfer hens to a dish, let rest for 5 minutes and then serve.

Nutrition Value:

- Calories: 173 Cal
- Fat: 7.4 g
- Carbs: 1 g
- Protein: 24.1 g
- Fiber: 0.2 g

BBQ Elk Short Ribs

Preparation time: 10 minutes
Cooking time: 1 hour
Servings: 6

Ingredients:

- 1/2 pound green beans
- 3 pounds elk short ribs
- 1/2 pound chanterelle mushrooms
- 6 ounces rib rub
- Salt as needed
- Ground black pepper as needed
- 4 tablespoons unsalted butter

Method:

1. Switch on the Traeger grill, fill the grill hopper with cherry flavored wood pellets, power the grill on by using the control panel, select 'smoke' on the temperature dial, or set the temperature to 275 degrees F and let it preheat for a minimum of 15 minutes.
2. Meanwhile, prepare the ribs, and for this, season them with salt and rib rub until well coated.
3. When the grill has preheated, open the lid, place ribs on the grill grate rib-side down, shut the grill and smoke for 30 minutes.
4. Then wrap ribs in foil in the double layer, return to the grill grate and continue smoking 15 minutes or until the internal temperature reaches 125 degrees.
5. When done, transfer ribs to a dish and let them rest until required.
6. Change the smoking temperature to 450 degrees F, shut with lid, and let it preheat for 15 minutes.
7. Then place a skillet pan on the grill grate and when hot, add butter and when it melts, add mushrooms and beans, toss until mixed, shut with lid, and cook for 15 minutes until vegetables have turned tender and golden brown.
8. Serve grilled vegetables with elk ribs.

Nutrition Value:

- Calories: 393 Cal
- Fat: 16.6 g
- Carbs: 25 g
- Protein: 36 g
- Fiber: 0.9 g

Grilled Duck Breast

Preparation time: 10 minutes
Cooking time: 20 minutes
Servings: 6

Ingredients:

- 4 duck breasts, boneless, each about 6 ounces
- 1/4 cup game rub

Method:

1. Switch on the Traeger grill, fill the grill hopper with cherry flavored wood pellets, power the grill on by using the control panel, select 'smoke' on the temperature dial, or set the temperature to 450 degrees F and let it preheat for a minimum of 15 minutes.
2. Meanwhile, score the skin of the duck breast in the form of the ¼-inch diamond pattern by using a sharp knife and then season with game rub until evenly coated.
3. When the grill has preheated, open the lid, place duck breasts on the grill grate skin-side down, shut the grill and smoke for 20 minutes until cooked and the internal temperature reaches 135 degrees F.
4. When done, transfer duck breasts to a cutting board, let them rest for 10 minutes, then cut into slices and then serve.

Nutrition Value:

- Calories: 220 Cal
- Fat: 18 g
- Carbs: 0 g
- Protein: 16 g
- Fiber: 0 g

Bison Slider

Preparation time: 10 minutes
Cooking time: 8 minutes
Servings: 8

Ingredients:

- 1 pound ground buffalo meat
- 1 tablespoon minced garlic
- 1 teaspoon salt
- 1 teaspoon ground black pepper
- 2 tablespoons Worcestershire sauce

Method:

1. Switch on the Traeger grill, fill the grill hopper with flavored wood pellets, power the grill on by using the control panel, select 'smoke' on the temperature dial, or set the temperature to 450 degrees F and let it preheat for a minimum of 5 minutes.
2. Meanwhile, take a medium bowl, place all the ingredients in it, stir until well combined, and then shape the mixture into eight patties.
3. When the grill has preheated, open the lid, place patties on the grill grate, shut the grill and smoke for 4 minutes per side until thoroughly cooked.
4. Serve patties with toasted buns and favorite toppings.

Nutrition Value:

- Calories: 120 Cal
- Fat: 8 g
- Carbs: 2 g
- Protein: 10 g
- Fiber: 0.6 g

Venison Rib Roast

Preparation time: 10 minutes
Cooking time: 25 minutes
Servings: 6

Ingredients:

- 2 pounds venison roast, about 8 ribs
- Rib rub as needed
- 1 tablespoon olive oil

Method:

1. Switch on the Traeger grill, fill the grill hopper with hickory flavored wood pellets, power the grill on by using the control panel, select 'smoke' on the temperature dial, or set the temperature to 375 degrees F and let it preheat for a minimum of 5 minutes.
2. Meanwhile, brush roast with oil and then season with rib rub until well coated.
3. When the grill has preheated, open the lid, place food on the grill grate, shut the grill, and smoke for 25 minutes until the internal temperature reaches 125 degrees F.
4. When done, transfer roast to a cutting board, let it rest for 10 minutes, then cut into slices and serve.

Nutrition Value:

- Calories: 128 Cal
- Fat: 2.8 g
- Carbs: 0 g
- Protein: 24.8 g
- Fiber: 0 g

Venison Meatloaf

Preparation time: 30 minutes
Cooking time: 1 hour and 15 minutes
Servings: 6

Ingredients:

For the Meatloaf:

- 1 medium white onion, peeled, diced
- 2 pounds ground venison
- 1 cup bread crumbs
- 1 teaspoon salt
- 1 tablespoon Worcestershire sauce
- ½ teaspoon ground black pepper
- 2 tablespoons onion soup mix
- 1 egg, beaten
- 1 cup milk, unsweetened

For the Glaze:

- 1/4 cup brown sugar
- 1/4 cup ketchup
- 1/4 cup apple cider vinegar

Method:

1. Switch on the Traeger grill, fill the grill hopper with big game blend wood pellets, power the grill on by using the control panel, select 'smoke' on the temperature dial, or set the temperature to 350 degrees F and let it preheat for a minimum of 15 minutes.
2. Meanwhile, take a large bowl, place all the ingredients for the meatloaf in it, and stir until just combined; don't overmix.
3. Take a loaf pan, grease it with oil, place meatloaf mixture in it, and spread evenly.
4. Prepare the glaze and for this, take a small bowl, place all of its ingredients in it, stir until combined, and then spread evenly on top of meatloaf.

5. When the grill has preheated, open the lid, place loaf pan on the grill grate, shut the grill and smoke for 1 hour and 15 minutes until the internal temperature reaches 165 degrees F.
6. Serve straight away.

Nutrition Value:

- Calories: 186.5 Cal
- Fat: 7.2 g
- Carbs: 7.7 g
- Protein: 21.6 g
- Fiber: 0.4 g

Chapter 10: Vegetable Recipes

Green Beans with Bacon

Preparation time. 10 minutes
Cooking time: 20 minutes
Servings: 6

Ingredients:

- 4 strips of bacon, chopped
- 1 1/2-pound green beans, ends trimmed
- 1 teaspoon minced garlic
- 1 teaspoon salt
- 4 tablespoons olive oil

Method:

1. Switch on the Traeger grill, fill the grill hopper with flavored wood pellets, power the grill on by using the control panel, select 'smoke' on the temperature dial, or set the temperature to 450 degrees F and let it preheat for a minimum of 15 minutes.
2. Meanwhile, take a sheet tray, place all the ingredients in it and toss until mixed.
3. When the grill has preheated, open the lid, place prepared sheet tray on the grill grate, shut the grill and smoke for 20 minutes until lightly browned and cooked.
4. When done, transfer green beans to a dish and then serve.

Nutrition Value:

- Calories: 93 Cal
- Fat: 4.6 g
- Carbs: 8.2 g
- Protein: 5.9 g
- Fiber: 2.9 g

Grilled Potato Salad

Preparation time: 15 minutes
Cooking time: 10 minutes
Servings: 8

Ingredients:

- 1 ½ pound fingerling potatoes, halved lengthwise
- 1 small jalapeno, sliced
- 10 scallions
- 2 teaspoons salt
- 2 tablespoons rice vinegar
- 2 teaspoons lemon juice
- 2/3 cup olive oil, divided

Method:

1. Switch on the Traeger grill, fill the grill hopper with pecan flavored wood pellets, power the grill on by using the control panel, select 'smoke' on the temperature dial, or set the temperature to 450 degrees F and let it preheat for a minimum of 5 minutes.
2. Meanwhile, prepare scallions, and for this, brush them with some oil.
3. When the grill has preheated, open the lid, place scallions on the grill grate, shut the grill and smoke for 3 minutes until lightly charred.
4. Then transfer scallions to a cutting board, let them cool for 5 minutes, then cut into slices and set aside until required.
5. Brush potatoes with some oil, season with some salt and black pepper, place potatoes on the grill grate, shut the grill and smoke for 5 minutes until thoroughly cooked.
6. Then take a large bowl, pour in remaining oil, add salt, lemon juice, and vinegar and stir until combined.
7. Add grilled scallion and potatoes, toss until well mixed, taste to adjust seasoning and then serve.

Nutrition Value:

- Calories: 223.7 Cal
- Fat: 12 g
- Carbs: 27 g
- Protein: 1.9 g
- Fiber: 3.3 g

Vegetable Sandwich

Preparation time: 30 minutes
Cooking time: 45 minutes
Servings: 4

Ingredients:

For the Smoked Hummus:

- 1 1/2 cups cooked chickpeas
- 1 tablespoon minced garlic
- 1 teaspoon salt
- 4 tablespoons lemon juice
- 2 tablespoon olive oil
- 1/3 cup tahini

For the Vegetables:

- 2 large portobello mushrooms
- 1 small eggplant, destemmed, sliced into strips
- 1 teaspoon salt
- 1 small zucchini, trimmed, sliced into strips
- ½ teaspoon ground black pepper
- 1 small yellow squash, peeled, sliced into strips
- ¼ cup olive oil

For the Cheese:

- 1 lemon, juiced
- ½ teaspoon minced garlic
- ¼ teaspoon ground black pepper
- ¼ teaspoon salt
- 1/2 cup ricotta cheese

To Assemble:

- 1 bunch basil, leaves chopped
- 2 heirloom tomatoes, sliced

- 4 ciabatta buns, halved

Method:

1. Switch on the Traeger grill, fill the grill hopper with pecan flavored wood pellets, power the grill on by using the control panel, select 'smoke' on the temperature dial, or set the temperature to 180 degrees F and let it preheat for a minimum of 15 minutes.
2. Meanwhile, prepare the hummus, and for this, take a sheet tray and spread chickpeas on it.
3. When the grill has preheated, open the lid, place sheet tray on the grill grate, shut the grill and smoke for 20 minutes.
4. When done, transfer chickpeas to a food processor, add remaining ingredients for the hummus in it, and pulse for 2 minutes until smooth, set aside until required.
5. Change the smoking temperature to 500 degrees F, shut with lid, and let it preheat for 10 minutes.
6. Meanwhile, prepare vegetables and for this, take a large bowl, place all the vegetables in it, add salt and black pepper, drizzle with oil and lemon juice and toss until coated.
7. Place vegetables on the grill grate, shut with lid and then smoke for eggplant, zucchini, and squash for 15 minutes and mushrooms for 25 minutes.
8. Meanwhile, prepare the cheese and for this, take a small bowl, place all of its ingredients in it and stir until well combined.
9. Assemble the sandwich for this, cut buns in half lengthwise, spread prepared hummus on one side, spread cheese on the other side, then stuff with grilled vegetables and top with tomatoes and basil.
10. Serve straight away.

Nutrition Value:

- Calories: 560 Cal
- Fat: 40 g
- Carbs: 45 g
- Protein: 8.3 g
- Fiber: 6.8 g

Grilled Zucchini

Preparation time: 5 minutes
Cooking time: 10 minutes
Servings: 6

Ingredients:

- 4 medium zucchinis
- 2 tablespoons olive oil
- 1 tablespoon sherry vinegar
- 2 sprigs of thyme, leaves chopped
- ½ teaspoon salt
- 1/3 teaspoon ground black pepper

Method:

1. Switch on the Traeger grill, fill the grill hopper with oak flavored wood pellets, power the grill on by using the control panel, select 'smoke' on the temperature dial, or set the temperature to 350 degrees F and let it preheat for a minimum of 5 minutes.
2. Meanwhile, cut the ends of each zucchini, cut each in half and then into thirds and place in a plastic bag.
3. Add remaining ingredients, seal the bag, and shake well to coat zucchini pieces.
4. When the grill has preheated, open the lid, place zucchini on the grill grate, shut the grill and smoke for 4 minutes per side.
5. When done, transfer zucchini to a dish, garnish with more thyme and then serve.

Nutrition Value:

- Calories: 74 Cal
- Fat: 5.4 g
- Carbs: 6.1 g
- Protein: 2.6 g
- Fiber: 2.3 g

Grilled Sugar Snap Peas

Preparation time: 15 minutes
Cooking time: 10 minutes
Servings: 4

Ingredients:

- 2-pound sugar snap peas, ends trimmed
- ½ teaspoon garlic powder
- 1 teaspoon salt
- 2/3 teaspoon ground black pepper
- 2 tablespoons olive oil

Method:

1. Switch on the Traeger grill, fill the grill hopper with apple-flavored wood pellets, power the grill on by using the control panel, select 'smoke' on the temperature dial, or set the temperature to 450 degrees F and let it preheat for a minimum of 15 minutes.
2. Meanwhile, take a medium bowl, place peas in it, add garlic powder and oil, season with salt and black pepper, toss until mixed and then spread on the sheet pan.
3. When the grill has preheated, open the lid, place the prepared sheet pan on the grill grate, shut the grill and smoke for 10 minutes until slightly charred.
4. Serve straight away.

Nutrition Value:

- Calories: 91 Cal
- Fat: 5 g
- Carbs: 9 g
- Protein: 4 g
- Fiber: 3 g

Cauliflower with Parmesan and Butter

Preparation time: 15 minutes
Cooking time: 45 minutes
Servings: 4

Ingredients:

- 1 medium head of cauliflower
- 1 teaspoon minced garlic
- 1 teaspoon salt
- ½ teaspoon ground black pepper
- 1/4 cup olive oil
- 1/2 cup melted butter, unsalted
- 1/2 tablespoon chopped parsley
- 1/4 cup shredded parmesan cheese

Method:

1. Switch on the Traeger grill, fill the grill hopper with flavored wood pellets, power the grill on by using the control panel, select 'smoke' on the temperature dial, or set the temperature to 450 degrees F and let it preheat for a minimum of 15 minutes.
2. Meanwhile, brush the cauliflower head with oil, season with salt and black pepper and then place in a skillet pan.
3. When the grill has preheated, open the lid, place prepared skillet pan on the grill grate, shut the grill and smoke for 45 minutes until golden brown and the center has turned tender.
4. Meanwhile, take a small bowl, place melted butter in it, and then stir in garlic, parsley, and cheese until combined.
5. Baste cheese mixture frequently in the last 20 minutes of cooking and, when done, remove the pan from heat and garnish cauliflower with parsley.
6. Cut it into slices and then serve.

Nutrition Value:

- Calories: 128 Cal
- Fat: 7.6 g
- Carbs: 10.8 g
- Protein: 7.4 g
- Fiber: 5 g

Grilled Carrots and Asparagus

Preparation time: 10 minutes
Cooking time: 30 minutes
Servings: 6

Ingredients:

- 1-pound whole carrots, with tops
- 1 bunch of asparagus, ends trimmed
- Sea salt as needed
- 1 teaspoon lemon zest
- 2 tablespoons honey
- 2 tablespoons olive oil

Method:

1. Switch on the Traeger grill, fill the grill hopper with flavored wood pellets, power the grill on by using the control panel, select 'smoke' on the temperature dial, or set the temperature to 450 degrees F and let it preheat for a minimum of 15 minutes.
2. Meanwhile, take a medium dish, place asparagus in it, season with sea salt, drizzle with oil and toss until mixed.
3. Take a medium bowl, place carrots in it, drizzle with honey, sprinkle with sea salt and toss until combined.
4. When the grill has preheated, open the lid, place asparagus and carrots on the grill grate, shut the grill and smoke for 30 minutes.
5. When done, transfer vegetables to a dish, sprinkle with lemon zest, and then serve.

Nutrition Value:

- Calories: 79.8 Cal
- Fat: 4.8 g
- Carbs: 8.6 g
- Protein: 2.6 g
- Fiber: 3.5 g

Kale Chips

Preparation time: 10 minutes
Cooking time: 20 minutes
Servings: 6

Ingredients:

- 2 bunches of kale, stems removed
- ½ teaspoon of sea salt
- 4 tablespoons olive oil

Method:

1. Switch on the Traeger grill, fill the grill hopper with apple-flavored wood pellets, power the grill on by using the control panel, select 'smoke' on the temperature dial, or set the temperature to 250 degrees F and let it preheat for a minimum of 15 minutes.
2. Meanwhile, rinse the kale leaves, pat dry, spread the kale on a sheet tray, drizzle with oil, season with salt and toss until well coated.
3. When the grill has preheated, open the lid, place sheet tray on the grill grate, shut the grill and smoke for 20 minutes until crisp.
4. Serve straight away.

Nutrition Value:

- Calories: 110 Cal
- Fat: 5 g
- Carbs: 15.8 g
- Protein: 5.3 g
- Fiber: 5.6 g

Roasted Root Vegetables

Preparation time: 15 minutes
Cooking time: 45 minutes
Servings: 6

Ingredients:

- 1 large red onion, peeled
- 1 bunch of red beets, trimmed, peeled
- 1 large yam, peeled
- 1 bunch of golden beets, trimmed, peeled
- 1 large parsnips, peeled
- 1 butternut squash, peeled
- 1 large carrot, peeled
- 6 garlic cloves, peeled
- 3 tablespoons thyme leaves
- Salt as needed
- 1 cinnamon stick
- Ground black pepper as needed
- 3 tablespoons olive oil
- 2 tablespoons honey

Method:

1. Switch on the Traeger grill, fill the grill hopper with hickory flavored wood pellets, power the grill on by using the control panel, select 'smoke' on the temperature dial, or set the temperature to 450 degrees F and let it preheat for a minimum of 15 minutes.
2. Meanwhile, cut all the vegetables into ½-inch pieces, place them in a large bowl, add garlic, thyme, and cinnamon, drizzle with oil and toss until mixed.
3. Take a large cookie sheet, line it with foil, spread with vegetables, and then season with salt and black pepper.
4. When the grill has preheated, open the lid, place prepared cookie sheet on the grill grate, shut the grill and smoke for 45 minutes until tender.
5. When done, transfer vegetables to a dish, drizzle with honey, and then serve.

Nutrition Value:

- Calories: 164 Cal
- Fat: 4 g
- Carbs: 31.7 g

- Protein: 2.7 g
- Fiber: 6.4 g

Vegetable Skewers

Preparation time: 10 minutes
Cooking time: 20 minutes
Servings: 4

Ingredients:

- 2 cups whole white mushrooms
- 2 large yellow squash, peeled, chopped
- 1 cup chopped pineapple
- 1 cup chopped red pepper
- 1 cup halved strawberries
- 2 large zucchinis, chopped

For the Dressing:

- 2 lemons, juiced
- ½ teaspoon ground black pepper
- 1/2 teaspoon sea salt
- 1 teaspoon red chili powder
- 1 tablespoon maple syrup
- 1 tablespoon orange zest
- 2 tablespoons apple cider vinegar
- 1/4 cup olive oil

Method:

1. Switch on the Traeger grill, fill the grill hopper with flavored wood pellets, power the grill on by using the control panel, select 'smoke' on the temperature dial, or set the temperature to 450 degrees F and let it preheat for a minimum of 5 minutes.
2. Meanwhile, prepared thread vegetables and fruits on skewers alternately and then brush skewers with oil.
3. When the grill has preheated, open the lid, place vegetable skewers on the grill grate, shut the grill, and smoke for 20 minutes until tender and lightly charred.
4. Meanwhile, prepare the dressing and for this, take a small bowl, place all of its ingredients in it and then whisk until combined.
5. When done, transfer skewers to a dish, top with prepared dressing and then serve.

Nutrition Value:

- Calories: 130 Cal
- Fat: 2 g
- Carbs: 20 g
- Protein: 2 g
- Fiber: 0.3 g

Conclusion

If you are considering buying a grill yourself, then first you need to know the best kind of grills out in the market and what will suit you. You need to know how they work, compare, and which ones are trending. Traeger wood pellet grill is top on the markets and has many advantages over the standard cooking grill everyone has. New technology is coming out with better and better products to choose from, and if you don't upgrade your purchase and keep buying the same old stuff, then you will be left behind.

The Traeger grill provides a person which a great barbecuing experience with everyone, making food tastes better and cooking easier.

Ingram Content Group UK Ltd.
Milton Keynes UK
UKHW030340210623
423783UK00008B/79